Muhlenberg County Public Librari
108 E. Broad Street
Central City, KY 42330

DATE DUE

GAYLORD   PRINTED IN U.S.A.

Ben Roethlisberger

FOOTBALL SUPERSTARS

Tiki Barber

Tom Brady

John Elway

Brett Favre

Peyton Manning

Dan Marino

Donovan McNabb

Joe Montana

Walter Payton

Jerry Rice

Ben Roethlisberger

Barry Sanders

FOOTBALL ⬤ SUPERSTARS

Ben Roethlisberger

Rachel A. Koestler-Grack

CHELSEA HOUSE
PUBLISHERS
An imprint of Infobase Publishing

BEN ROETHLISBERGER

Chelsea House
An imprint of Infobase Publishing
132 West 31st Street
New York NY 10001

Library of Congress Cataloging-in-Publication Data
Koestler-Grack, Rachel A., 1973-
  Ben Roethlisberger / by Rachel A. Koestler-Grack.
     p. cm. -- (Football superstars)
  Includes bibliographical references and index.
  ISBN 978-0-7910-9837-0 (hardcover)
  1. Roethlisberger, Ben, 1982---Juvenile literature. 2. Football players--United States--Biography--Juvenile literature. I. Title. II. Series.

  GV939.R623K64 2008
  796.332092--dc22
  [B]
                          2008012411

Chelsea House books are available at special discounts when purchased in bulk quantities for businesses, associations, institutions, or sales promotions. Please call our Special Sales Department in New York at (212) 967-8800 or (800) 322-8755.

You can find Chelsea House on the World Wide Web at http://www.chelseahouse.com

Text design by Erik Lindstrom
Cover design by Ben Peterson

Printed in the United States of America

Bang EJB 10 9 8 7 6 5 4 3 2

This book is printed on acid-free paper.

All links and Web addresses were checked and verified to be correct at the time of publication. Because of the dynamic nature of the Web, some addresses and links may have changed since publication and may no longer be valid.

CONTENTS

Big Ben Delivers an XL Win

On February 5, 2006, the crowd at Ford Field in Detroit, Michigan, was ready to burst. Even though the Pittsburgh Steelers were far from home, the sea of yellow "Terrible Towels" in the stands told them otherwise. For one Steeler—running back Jerome "The Bus" Bettis, this was home. He was born and raised in Detroit, and he had come home for his final NFL game—Super Bowl XL. The only trouble was that second-year **quarterback** Ben Roethlisberger, aka Big Ben, had not been putting on the show the fans had hoped to see. Instead, he was playing more like the 23-year-old quarterback he was.

The Seattle Seahawks had dominated the first quarter. Roethlisberger finished the quarter with a string of incomplete passes, and Pittsburgh was behind 3-0. In the second quarter, however, the pendulum started to swing. It was a seemingly modest play that changed the course of the game. With a little less than nine minutes left in the half, Steelers **cornerback** Deshea Townsend cut down Seattle fullback Mack Strong on a **swing pass** six inches shy of a **first down**. Pittsburgh got the ball back but only gained four yards on the first two plays. On third and 6 at the Steelers' 45-yard line, Roethlisberger tucked the ball down and ducked under a defender before spotting his favorite wide receiver—Hines Ward. He tossed a **shovel pass** to Ward for a 12-yard gain. Two plays later, Cedrick Wilson found an opening downfield, and Roethlisberger connected with him for another 20 yards.

After a penalty and a **sack**, the Steelers were sitting on third and 28 at the Seattle 40 when they pulled out the biggest and craziest play of the first half. In all common sense, a safe 10-yard play would have put the Steelers in comfortable field-goal range. The play they ran, though, took a slightly different spin. Flushed out of the **pocket**, Roethlisberger seemed to be on the verge of scrambling the distance. Just inches short of the **line of scrimmage**, though, Roethlisberger ran sideways. He spotted Ward streaking downfield and launched the football across the field. Beating strong safety Michael Boulware to the ball, Ward grabbed the pass for a 37-yard gain to Seattle's 3-yard line. Two handoffs to Bettis left Pittsburgh one yard short of a **touchdown**. On the next play, Roethlisberger rolled left, faked a pitch to Bettis, and kept the ball. He cut back toward the middle and leaped to the **end zone**, crashing into linebacker D.D. Lewis. Even though Lewis knocked Roethlisberger backward, the play was ruled a touchdown, because the ball had crossed the **plane** of the goal line. With 1:55 remaining in the first half, the Steelers took a 7-3 lead.

STILL MORE THEATRICS

As it turned out, Pittsburgh's made-for-the-big-screen offense had an encore planned in the second half. Clenching a 14-10 lead in the fourth quarter, the Steelers had the ball on Seattle's

Pittsburgh Steelers quarterback Ben Roethlisberger dove in for a one-yard touchdown in the second quarter of Super Bowl XL on February 5, 2006, in Detroit. The touchdown gave the Steelers a 7-3 lead over the Seattle Seahawks. In only his second season in the National Football League, Roethlisberger had led his team to the game's biggest stage.

43-yard line. Roethlisberger handed off to Willie Parker, who quickly handed the ball to wide receiver Antwaan Randle El as he was rushing right. Meanwhile, Ward had looped downfield into the open, and Randle El, who was a record-setting college quarterback at Indiana University, hit Ward in stride for a 43-yard touchdown with 9:04 remaining in the game. The score was all the Steelers needed. The Seahawks had no answer for Pittsburgh, who made Super-Bowl-winning history with their 21-10 victory.

For the fifth time in franchise history, the Steelers had taken a Super Bowl title, tying them with the Dallas Cowboys and the San Francisco 49ers. It was an extra-large—XL—win for the Steelers and the Rooney family (the owners of the Steelers), bringing the Lombardi Trophy back to Pittsburgh after 26 years of waiting. In only his second year in the league,

HISTORY OF THE PITTSBURGH STEELERS

The Pittsburgh Steelers are part of the North Division of the American Football Conference (AFC North). They are the oldest franchise in the AFC and have also won the most championships—appearing in six Super Bowls and winning five. Originally named the Pirates, Pittsburgh joined the NFL in 1933. The Steelers are descendents of the first-ever pro-football team, as Pittsburgh hosted the world's first pro game in the 1880s. That early franchise, though, fell victim to Pennsylvania's "blue laws," which (before 1933) prohibited sporting events from being played on Sundays.

In 1940, the franchise was reformed and renamed the Pittsburgh Steelers, because of the city's prominence in the steel industry. A fan had suggested the name in a contest held by the team and the *Pittsburgh Post-Gazette*. For several decades, the Steelers were a mediocre team that rarely made the playoffs. In 1970, when the American Football League merged with the National Football League, the Steelers were one of three NFL teams to switch to the newly formed American Football Conference, which consisted of the original AFL teams.

During the 1970s, under head coach Chuck Noll, the Steelers finally became winners. Noll had a knack for spotting football stars and making remarkable draft selections,

Roethlisberger became the youngest quarterback in NFL history to win the Super Bowl. On top of that, the Steelers were the first team ever to enter the postseason as a No. 6 **seed** in the conference playoffs and win three road games en route to the Super Bowl. They defied the odds to get there and came out on top.

such as taking Hall of Famers "Mean" Joe Greene in 1969, Terry Bradshaw and Mel Blount in 1970, Jack Ham in 1971, and Franco Harris in 1972. In 1974, he picked a Hall-of-Fame buffet by drafting Mike Webster, Lynn Swann, John Stallworth, and Jack Lambert all in one year. The Pittsburgh Steelers' 1974 draft has gone down in NFL history as the best ever. No other team has ever drafted four future Hall of Famers in one year. These players formed one of the NFL's greatest football dynasties, making the playoffs in eight seasons and becoming the only team to win four Super Bowls in six years, as well as the first to win more than two.

As those players retired, the Steelers suffered a bit of a slump in the 1980s. When the Chuck Noll era ended after the 1991 season, the Bill Cowher era began. Cowher took the team to the playoffs in each of his first six seasons. The Steelers lost Super Bowl XXX to Dallas but 10 years later, won Super Bowl XL over Seattle. After 15 years with the team, Cowher stepped down as coach at the end of the 2006 season. Current coach Mike Tomlin has big shoes to fill and high expectations to meet. But he is off to a promising start, making the playoffs during his first season. Someone else in Pittsburgh started out the same way—he is known by most as Big Ben.

Roethlisberger did not play his best game, completing only 9 of 21 passes with two **interceptions**, but he helped make plays when the Steelers needed them most. "We got the win, and that's all that matters," he said after the game, as quoted by the Associated Press. The Steelers had not been a one-man team. Roethlisberger shared his offensive duties with a killer running game and competent receivers. Likewise, the Steelers defense was its usual hard-hitting force. Time and time again, Roethlisberger displayed humility and gave credit where credit was due. After the Super Bowl, Big Ben was asked if he was thankful that his supporting cast had played well enough to win. "They're not my supporting cast," he answered, as quoted in *The Washington Post*. "I'm their supporting cast. Two interceptions—that's the recipe for disaster—yet we won. I've bragged on these guys all year and always will."

The season before, when veteran Tommy Maddox was sidelined with an injury, Roethlisberger—a fresh-off-the-**draft** rookie—slid into his position as the starting quarterback with incredible ease and a confidence that quickly earned the respect of his teammates. With a calmness that typically comes only with age, Big Ben led the Steelers to the AFC Championship Game that year. Pittsburgh's loss to the New England Patriots that day was Roethlisberger's first loss in 15 games as an NFL starter. Roethlisberger finished his **rookie** season as the No. 5 quarterback in the NFL, with a **passer rating** of 98.1. He was voted the Associated Press NFL Offensive Rookie of the Year and the *Sporting News* Rookie of the Year.

Big Ben hit the NFL blazing, and he intends on continuing as one of the league's top quarterbacks. The clean-cut kid from the small, blue-collar town of Findlay, Ohio, now has sandwiches named after him at local Pittsburgh diners. Teammate Hines Ward said the words that everyone in the NFL had been thinking ever since Roethlisberger rolled into Pittsburgh, "One game away as a rookie and he wins the Super Bowl in the second year? Imagine that—and there are so many years left."

Rise Above
the Rest

On March 2, 1982, in the small Ohio town of Findlay, Ben was born to Ken and Ida Roethlisberger. When Ben was about two years old, Ken and Ida Roethlisberger divorced. Young Ben lived primarily with his father, who quickly remarried. Ben loved his new stepmother, Brenda, and the family soon grew bigger when his sister, Carlee, was born. When Ben was 8 years old, tragedy struck as his mother, Ida, was suddenly killed in a car accident. Surrounded by a loving family, Ben learned to deal with the pain of losing his mother, but he never forgot her. Even today, he still points heavenward after each touchdown, knowing that his mom is up there watching him.

At a young age, Ben became active in sports, and he had exceptional talent in basketball and football. He and his friends got together in one another's yards to emulate their NFL heroes. Pretending it was the Super Bowl, they would throw the ball as Joe Montana and catch passes as Jerry Rice. Ben's biggest idols were Montana, the 49ers quarterback, and John Elway, the Denver Broncos quarterback. Whenever he could, Ben would take Elway's uniform number—No. 7—in any sport he played, all the way up to the pros. Ben's athletic gifts and natural abilities were apparent to anyone who watched him play. "Some kids just rise above the rest, and Ben was one of them," commented Tony Iriti, the mayor of Findlay, on Roethlisberger's Web site, BigBen7.com. Iriti was Ben's fifth- and sixth-grade football coach and a volunteer assistant at Findlay High School. "You usually don't expect a kid to make every play, but Ben always seemed to make things work," he said.

A thin and lanky teenager, Ben played **wideout** for the Findlay High School Trojans. It was not until the fall of 1999—Ben's senior year—that he finally earned the chance to be the No. 1 quarterback after the previous starting quarterback graduated. His years as a receiver helped him understand coverage schemes from the defense. Ben did not let his years backstage slow him down. In the 1999 season, he led the Trojans to a 10–2 record and to the second round of the state playoffs in Ohio, before losing to Grove City. During the regular season, Ben passed for 4,041 yards and 54 touchdowns, both state records. That year, he participated in the Ohio North-South and Ohio-Pennsylvania Big 33 games, in which he threw for two touchdowns, including the game-winner in the North-South game. He was named the Ohio Division I Offensive Player of the Year for 1999 and was runner-up for the 1999 Mr. Football honors in Ohio.

During his high school years, Ben was not just burning up the field in football. His talents glittered in other sports as well. He was named an all-league player in baseball and basketball. In all three sports, he served as team captain. As a point guard in basketball, he averaged 26.5 points, 9 rebounds, and 5 assists a game during his senior year. Ben also set the school's career

A giant poster of Ben Roethlisberger, featuring his high school team picture, was put up on a building in downtown Findlay, Ohio, just before Super Bowl XL in 2006. In high school, Roethlisberger had to wait for three years behind the starting quarterback. He did not get the chance to be Findlay High's No. 1 quarterback until his senior year.

scoring record in basketball. As shortstop for the Findlay baseball team, he was a .300 hitter.

Even though his quarterbacking talent had remained hidden for his first three years of high school, Ben was able to attract attention from college football teams. Just before his senior year, his explosive abilities became apparent to the football staff at Miami University in Oxford, Ohio, who invited him to summer camp before his senior year. At camp, he performed well but left without a scholarship. After all, Ben had not yet played one game as a starting quarterback. Miami head coach Terry Hoeppner worried that some people might think he was foolish to offer a scholarship to a kid who had not even played one game at No. 1. In Ben's first game as quarterback at Findlay High, he threw six touchdowns. "That's good enough for me," Hoeppner said.

After seeing what Ben could do, Ohio State University, from the more prestigious Big Ten Conference, also tried to woo him with a scholarship. But Ben went with Miami of Ohio. His state records for touchdowns and passing yardage came while playing a high-power offense similar to the one Miami ran. Also, Ohio State had him slotted as a **tight end**. "It came down to what felt right," Roethlisberger later said on his Web site. "I prayed a lot about it, talked to my family about it, and [Miami] seemed like the right fit." So, in the spring of 2000, Ben graduated from Findlay High School, anticipating his career as a Miami RedHawk.

CAPTURING A MAC TITLE

As a freshman in 2000, Ben was a RedHawk **redshirt**, meaning that he sat out the first year so that he would have four more years of eligibility to play. He took over as the starting quarterback in the 2001 season. In his first two games against Michigan and Iowa, Ben struggled. His blunders, though, quickly disappeared. During the first home game, against rival Cincinnati, Ben completed 20 of 25 passes for 264 yards, two touchdowns, and a RedHawk victory. In his first season as the starting quarterback, he threw for an impressive 3,105 yards, with 25 touchdowns and 13 interceptions. He set school records with his passing yards and number of touchdowns. Three times, he was named the Mid-American Conference (MAC) Player of the Week, and at the end of the season, he was named the conference's Freshman of the Year.

Also in his first season, Roethlisberger acquired the nickname that has stayed with him into his pro career. Seconds were ticking away toward the end of a game against the University of Akron. To give Miami the win, Roethlisberger had to heave a 70-yard **Hail Mary** touchdown pass. The play he ran was called "Big Ben"—and from then on, the nickname stuck.

His second season at Miami, in 2002, was equally strong, with 3,238 passing yards, 22 touchdowns, and just 11 interceptions.

Ben Roethlisberger gets off a pass in the fourth quarter of the Mid-American Conference championship game in December 2003. With Roethlisberger in command of the offense, the 2003 Miami RedHawks won 11 straight games after a season-opening loss to Iowa.

He became only the fourth quarterback in the history of the conference to record two seasons with more than 3,000 passing yards. Ben had other talents on the football field, too, filling in for Miami's injured punter. He drilled nine of 11 punts inside the opponent's 20-yard line.

By his junior year, Ben had complete command of the offense. According to Coach Hoeppner, Ben took a "quantum leap" forward during the 2003 season. After an opening-game loss at Iowa, Ben dominated the field. He completed nearly 70 percent of his passes, and rewrote almost every Miami passing record—some of which were his own. The RedHawks plowed through the season, toppling every other team they played,

ENTRANCE EXAMS

Getting accepted into the NFL is kind of like getting accepted into a top-notch college. Draftees may not have to take another ACT or SAT, but they still need to bring their No. 2 lead pencils. And, of course, they need to demonstrate their athleticism. Every February, prospective players head to the NFL Scouting Combine, where they undertake physical and mental tests in front of NFL coaches, general managers, and scouts. How athletes perform at the Combine can be critical to their football careers. Players get ratings in the following tests: 40-yard dash, vertical jump, broad jump, bench press, pro agility shuttle, three-cone agility, and 60-yard shuttle.

Some of Ben's Combine ratings were 4.75 seconds in the 40-yard dash; 340 pounds in bench press; and 32 inches in the vertical jump. Roethlisberger's speed was impressive. Most running-back draftees run the 40-yard dash between 4.4 and 4.8 seconds. For a quarterback, Big Ben was fast.

winning 11 straight games to earn the right to play in the Mid-American Conference championship game.

On December 4, 2003, the RedHawks battled the Bowling Green Falcons for the MAC title. The game started out tight. Early in the first half, Bowling Green blocked a Miami punt, recovering the ball at Miami's 33-yard line and setting up the first touchdown. Bowling Green led 7-0 with 11:46 left in the opening quarter. Five plays later, Ben answered with a 53-yard touchdown pass. Once more, the Falcons jumped ahead, but Miami was quick to even the score.

Miami did not take the lead until late in the second quarter. On the play, Ben sidestepped a **blitzing** defender, rolled left,

Football players have to be more than just quick on their feet, however. They also have to think quickly. When a play unfolds, it can be unpredictable. A player in any position must be able to think creatively and improvise. Players also must learn and execute complex plays, and remember plenty of them. To measaure their abilities in this area, NFL draftees take a type of intelligence test called the Wonderlic. This 50-question IQ test starts with relatively easy questions such as: "In the following set of words, which word is different from the others? 1) copper, 2) nickel, 3) aluminum, 4) wood, 5) bronze." The questions get more difficult, such as: "A rectangular bin, completely filled, holds 640 cubic feet of grain. If the bin is 8 feet wide and 10 feet long, how deep is it?" A score of 10 is considered basic literacy—in other words, not too smart. Most NFL players score in the 20s. The only NFL player to score a perfect 50 was former Bengals punter and Harvard graduate Pat McInally. Roethlisberger scored a 25.

and nailed receiver Mike Larkin with a 16-yard touchdown pass. With 4:36 remaining in the first half, Miami led 21-14. At halftime, the Falcons trailed by only 21-17, even though Miami had outgained them 306 yards to 172 yards.

Early in the second half, the Falcons fell apart and never recovered. Back-to-back **fumbles** gave the RedHawks the ball inside Falcon territory each time. Ben took advantage of each possession, striking with two touchdowns—a one-yard plunge and a 13-yard carry. With 4:57 to go in the third quarter, Miami held a commanding 35-17 lead.

Ben sealed a RedHawk victory with a 55-yard touchdown pass to Calvin Murray. With 17 seconds left in the third quarter, Miami was up 42-20. In the fourth quarter, both teams added a touchdown, but the night belonged to Ben and the RedHawks. With a final score of 49-27, Miami won its first MAC title since 1986. Ben, who was the MAC player of the year, completed 26 of 35 passes for a record-setting 440 passing yards; he threw seven touchdowns to four receivers.

Bowling Green had had no answer for Ben. He was on target all night, whether he threw short or deep passes. He picked apart the defense, spreading the ball among nine receivers. After the game, Ben humbly gave the credit to his teammates. "All I had to do was put it out there and they made the play," he said, as quoted in *Roethlisberger: Pittsburgh's Own Big Ben*. He further praised his **offensive line** for not allowing a single sack. "I still have a white jersey," he said and grinned. On defense, Miami brought Bowling Green's short passing game to a screeching halt and put the pressure on Falcon quarterback Josh Harris.

SPECULATION ABOUT THE FUTURE

After the championship game, people wondered if Ben would return to Miami for the 2004 season or enter the NFL draft. If he chose to enter the draft, he was projected to be a top pick. For the moment, Ben remained quiet about the issue. He was more concerned about the GMAC Bowl on December 18, which the victory over Bowling Green had secured for Miami. There, the RedHawks trampled Louisville 49-28. Roethlisberger threw for 376 yards and four first-half touchdowns. The victory gave Miami a 13–1 record and the longest winning streak of any major college football team. The RedHawks finished at No. 10 in the final Associated Press poll of the season.

In 14 games during the 2003 season, Ben passed for a conference-record 4,486 yards with 37 touchdowns and only 10 interceptions. With his season performance, he became a semifinalist for the Davey O'Brien Award, which is given to the top quarterback in the nation.

Ben's No. 1 goal had always been to win a championship. After the RedHawks beat Louisville, he felt as if he had accomplished all he had wanted to in college football. His ambition switched gears. On December 18, after the GMAC Bowl, Ben announced that he would file for the NFL draft. "I feel the time is right to embark on the next challenge," he said, according to an article by the Associated Press. "I'll always be grateful for the wonderful experiences of the past four years." The once-lanky teenager now stood a towering 6 feet 5 inches (196 centimeters) and weighed a hefty 240 pounds (109 kilograms). His strong arm was legendary, and he moved with an athleticism rare for his bulky size. Some team was sure to snatch up this gem of a quarterback. The question was merely who it would be.

First-Round Pick

Entering the NFL draft is not a simple waiting game. No matter how well a player performs on the college field, he still has to showcase his worthiness, polishing his physical appearance and athletic attributes until they shine like a new penny. When Ben Roethlisberger decided to leave Miami of Ohio after his junior year, he did not realize just how much his life was about to change. He waved good-bye to final exams, midnight runs to Taco Bell, and even Midwest winter storms. He was on his way to sunny Newport Beach, California, where he would overhaul his diet, take on a rigid workout schedule, and learn the social graces of an NFL quarterback.

Preparing for the draft was more exhausting than a full-time job. Nearly every day, Roethlisberger spent an hour in weight training, an hour or more working with a quarterback coach to tighten his throwing motion, and another hour working to improve his speed. In addition to the physical training, he visited his agent daily to do interviews, get his mail, and attend to other matters. Sunday was Roethlisberger's only day off. "I had an idea it would be tough, but I didn't know how tough," he said in *Roethlisberger: Pittsburgh's Own Big Ben*. "I didn't know how much time I had to put into it."

The draft holds high stakes. In 2003, first-round draft picks snatched $210 million in **signing bonuses**. Moving up just a few spots in the draft could reel in millions of dollars. In 2004, Roethlisberger, Eli Manning, and Philip Rivers were considered the top quarterbacks in the draft. Pedestal quarterbacks get the big bucks but also carry heavy expectations. "The stakes for a player like Ben are much higher, and the dynamic is different than it would be for a typical player," Roethlisberger's agent, Leigh Steinberg, pointed out in *Pittsburgh's Own Big Ben*.

In the weeks leading up to the draft, Roethlisberger worked out at various scouting combines. Steinberg took him to the Senior Bowl to make him a familiar face among NFL scouts, coaches, and general managers. In February, Roethlisberger accompanied Steinberg to Super Bowl XXXVIII at Reliant Stadium in Houston, Texas, hoping to get a taste for the mass media. There, he was starstruck when he saw some of his childhood football heroes, like Ronnie Lott, Joe Montana, Howie Long, Cris Carter, and Warren Moon. "I had posters of these guys," Roethlisberger said in an Associated Press article. At first, the whole pre-draft experience was a bit overwhelming. It did not take long, however, for Roethlisberger to settle into his prospective future. "It's starting to sink in that this is kind of my life now and it's going to be my life," he said.

In the 2004 draft, Roethlisberger was the third quarterback chosen, after Manning (the top pick) and Rivers (the fourth overall pick). The Pittsburgh Steelers drafted Roethlisberger in the first round with the eleventh pick. Roethlisberger was only the second quarterback drafted in the first round by the Steelers

The Pittsburgh Steelers chose Ben Roethlisberger with the eleventh pick in the first round of the NFL Draft on April 24, 2004. Here, after the pick was announced, Roethlisberger held up a Steelers jersey. He was the third quarterback overall selected in the draft.

in 33 years. Coach Bill Cowher saw that Roethlisberger's athleticism was too great a prize to let slip away. "If you have an opportunity to get a good, young quarterback who has a tremendous upside, it's too golden an opportunity to pass," he said, as quoted on Roethlisberger's Web site.

Although Roethlisberger never criticized Manning or Rivers, he believed that he had a little more to offer than either of them. Eli Manning, the younger brother of Indianapolis Colts star quarterback Peyton Manning, received a lot of press attention before the draft. Some claimed that Eli's family lineage—besides his brother, his father, Archie, was an NFL quarterback for 14 seasons—gave him an edge over other quarterbacks in the draft. Roethlisberger, however, was never sucked into the hype. "It all boils down to this," he said in an Associated Press article, "it's just football. Once I get on the field, my will to win is much greater than both of them."

When he arrived in Pittsburgh in April, though, Roethlisberger was still No. 3—on the Steelers' **depth chart**. At first glance, it seemed that he would have to wait a little longer to prove his passion than Manning would with the New York Giants or Rivers would with the San Diego Chargers. In the meantime, he was ready to learn as much as he could from Steelers starting quarterback Tommy Maddox and backup Charlie Batch. Perhaps the Steelers secretly underestimated Roethlisberger's potential. At least they did his size, when they handed him a much-too-small No. 7 jersey for his first photo shoot. Maddox, though, understood that Roethlisberger and the contract he would receive would have an impact on Maddox's position with the team. Maddox knew that he might be playing the 2004 season only for the chance to earn a spot with a different team in 2005.

On August 4, 2004, Roethlisberger signed a six-year, $40 million contract with Pittsburgh—becoming the highest-paid Steeler in history. No team dishes out that kind of money for a quarterback to stand on the sidelines for very long. Roethlisberger's agent, Leigh Steinberg, believed that he was worth every penny. "This is a franchise quarterback," he said in an article by the Associated Press. "I think he's a Troy Aikman, John Elway type of quarterback. He's that good." Roethlisberger's contract consisted of $22,269,500 in salary and bonuses. He also pulled down $17,730,500 in incentives, including $4,875,000 in playing-time bonuses that would be easy for a starting quarterback to achieve. His base salary for his rookie year was $230,000 and increased with each year of his contract—$305,000 in 2005, $655,000 in 2006, $1,026,000 in 2007, $1,356,000 in 2008, and $1,707,000 in 2009. He would get a $500,000 bonus if he made the Pro Bowl and an additional $4,750,000 for finishing in the top five of various statistical categories. He could tack on as much as $975,000 each year if the Steelers made the playoffs.

This contract would undoubtedly boost Roethlisberger from No. 3 to backup quarterback, but he was not expected to move into the starting spot until 2005. He kept a level head about the whole situation. "Now that the contract's out of the way, it's time for football. I'm ready to do whatever is asked of me, whether it's be the backup or play third string." he said, as quoted in *Roethlisberger: Pittsburgh's Own Big Ben.*

At training camp, Roethlisberger had to play a little catch-up, because he missed the first four practices while ironing out the details of his contract. He was extremely nervous as he stepped onto the field on his first day. In the stands, 10,000 expectant eyes were glued to his every move. On the first play, he lined up under center at the 20-yard line in a 7-on-7 passing drill. He was so excited that he overthrew his first pass to wide receiver Plaxico Burress. On the next play, he threaded a pass through heavy coverage, hitting Burress at the 1. Just like that, the butterflies flittered away. He knew that, once he got that first play out of the way, he would settle into the groove of the game. For the rest of the day, he displayed tremendous confidence, arm strength, and in-huddle leadership.

Although the Steelers did not plan to rush Roethlisberger onto the field during his rookie year, they would have a difficult time keeping him on the bench for long if he kept up his consistency in practice. For the time being, though, the only way Roethlisberger would find his way into the huddle was if Maddox suffered an injury or played exceptionally poorly. Even under those circumstances, backup Charlie Batch might still get the call.

GETTING WET

The second week of the 2004 season—Sunday, September 19—Roethlisberger stood on the sidelines at M&T Bank Stadium in Baltimore, Maryland. In the third quarter, the Ravens held a 13-0 lead over the Steelers. Maddox had completed just 4 of 13 passes for a meager 67 yards. Then, a powerful hit from Baltimore cornerback Gary Baxter took Maddox out of the game with an elbow injury. Maddox fumbled on the sack, and Baltimore scored on the following play to give the Ravens a 20-0 lead. Suddenly, Roethlisberger found himself making his NFL debut, much earlier than he had ever anticipated.

Roethlisberger had a rocky start. On his second possession, he threw an interception to Baltimore's Adalius Thomas. Luckily, the error did not result in another touchdown. Instead, the Ravens were forced to punt. The two teams traded possessions for the rest of the third quarter without scoring.

Finally in the fourth quarter, the game started to fall into place for Roethlisberger and the Steelers. To start out the quarter, Roethlisberger completed a pass to Duce Staley for nine yards. Next, he hit Hines Ward for a 58-yard gain to the 3-yard line. On second down, Roethlisberger connected with Antwaan Randle El on a touchdown pass. Kicker Jeff Reed's **extra point** was good, putting Pittsburgh on the board 20-7. The Ravens answered with a 49-yard drive that ended in a **field goal**. The kickoff return left Pittsburgh at its own 30-yard line. Roethlisberger drove the ball 70 yards, finishing with a pass to

Ben Roethlisberger celebrated after throwing the first touchdown of his career, in a game against the Baltimore Ravens on September 19, 2004. Roethlisberger entered the game after starting quarterback Tommy Maddox injured his elbow. The injury was expected to sideline Maddox for six weeks, so Roethlisberger was going to be Pittsburgh's starting quarterback much sooner than expected.

Ward for a 12-yard touchdown. The Steelers were closing the gap, 23-13. Pittsburgh decided to go for a **two-point conversion**, but Roethlisberger's pass attempt to Burress failed.

The Pittsburgh defense managed to hold the Ravens scoreless on their next possession, but the Steelers' luck soon ran dry. With 2:56 remaining in the game, Roethlisberger threw an interception to Baltimore's Chris McAlister. McAlister ran the ball back 51 yards for a touchdown, widening the spread to a nearly impossible 29-13 lead. The extra point was good, and time ran out for the Steelers. The 30-13 loss, however, was not as crushing as it could have been, considering the score was 20-0 going into the fourth quarter and Roethlisberger was facing a solid defense. Roethlisberger received some valuable real-game experience, completing 12 of 20 passes for 176 yards, two touchdowns, and two interceptions. "I'd say I got my feet wet, but I got my whole leg wet," Roethlisberger said after the game, according to the Associated Press. "It's tough, you come out and your first game is against probably one of, if not the best, defense in the NFL."

An examination after the game showed that Maddox had **ligament** and **tendon** tears in his right elbow. He would be out for at least six weeks. Once doctors cleared him to throw, the Steelers would then have to decide when he could play again. In the meantime, Roethlisberger was their No. 1 guy. While Roethlisberger was eager to prove his talent, his teammates knew that the transition would take extra work on their part as well. Co-captain and All-Pro offensive guard Alan Faneca seemed less than thrilled about the rookie leading the Pittsburgh pack. In an interview with the *Pittsburgh Post-Gazette*, soon after Roethlisberger's debut, Faneca said, "No, it's not exciting. Do you want to go work with some little young kid who's just out of college? Everybody's got to do a little more . . . put the extra work in this week and rally around him and help out."

Roethlisberger did not take Faneca's comments personally. He understood that his teammates would have to step up. Coach Bill Cowher had planned to bring Roethlisberger along gradually, expecting that he would have time to learn the

Steelers' system. Roethlisberger was not yet totally familiar with the offense. His biggest adjustment during his six-week role as a fill-in would be getting comfortable as a conventional drop-back quarterback. In college, Roethlisberger worked more than 50 percent of his snaps out of a **shotgun offense** and had his best success throwing on the run. Against the Ravens, because

THE BEST YOUNG GUN

Besides Ben Roethlisberger, several young quarterbacks had breakout years in 2004. Roethlisberger, though, edged out Byron Leftwich as the best of these quarterbacks (all first-round draft picks), according to a 2004 poll of three NFL pro person-nel directors published in November in the *Sporting News*. The scouts were asked to rate five quarterbacks in each of nine cat-egories on a scale of 1 to 10 points, with 10 being the highest. Here is how the quarterbacks were rated:

	BEN ROETHLISBERGER	BYRON LEFTWICH	DAVID CARR
Drafted	2004 #11 Pittsburgh	2003 #7 Jacksonville	2002 #1 Houston
Accuracy	7.7	8.0	7.3
Arm strength	8.0	8.3	8.7
Decision making	8.0	7.7	7.0
Footwork	8.3	6.0	8.0
Leadership	7.7	9.3	7.7
Mobility	7.7	5.7	8.3
Poise	8.3	9.0	8.0
Understanding of offense	7.3	8.3	8.0
Ability to win	8.7	8.7	7.3
TOTAL	71.7	71.0	70.3

the team was already so far behind, he played from the shot-gun. The following Sunday in Miami, he would not have that luxury. He was prepared, though, to make the most of his early opportunity. "I've got to be the leader now," he said.

In Miami on September 26, Roethlisberger stared down a string of bad omens. The tail of Hurricane Jeanne forced

	JOEY HARRINGTON	CARSON PALMER
Drafted	2002 #3	2003 #1
	Detroit	Cincinnati
Accuracy	7.0	7.0
Arm strength	7.0	8.0
Decision making	7.0	6.0
Footwork	7.7	7.7
Leadership	7.3	6.3
Mobility	7.3	6.7
Poise	6.7	7.0
Understanding of offense	8.0	7.0
Ability to win	6.3	6.0
TOTAL	**64.3**	**61.7**

It is interesting to note that, going into the 2008 season, only Roethlisberger and Palmer remain with the teams that drafted them. Harrington played for the Miami Dolphins in 2006 and joined the Atlanta Falcons in 2007. Leftwich also played for the Falcons in 2007. He was released in February 2008 and had yet to sign with another team. Carr spent 2007 with the Carolina Panthers and signed with the New York Giants in 2008 to be a backup.

In his first start as an NFL quarterback, Ben Roethlisberger had to guide his team through torrential downpours on a sloppy field as the tail of Hurricane Jeanne passed over Miami. Here, he scrambles out of the pocket during the third quarter. Roethlisberger showed the poise of a veteran, though, leading Pittsburgh to a 13-3 win over the Dolphins on September 26, 2004.

a seven-and-a-half-hour delay of the game and a loss of power at the team hotel. In his first game as an NFL starter, Roethlisberger stepped onto a soggy field and clenched a slippery ball. First-half downpours made holding onto the ball tricky for both teams. Miami fumbled on its first possession, and Roethlisberger took over at the Dolphins' 30-yard line. His first pass was intercepted by Miami's Patrick Surtain, but Pittsburgh's defense snatched it back with an interception of its own. From the Steelers' 20-yard line, Roethlisberger **moved the chains** in an eight-play, 58-yard drive for a 40-yard field goal.

The rest of the first half featured a circus of events—Pittsburgh missed two field-goal attempts, and Miami had a punt blocked and another pass intercepted—all as mud-smeared players waded through a field ankle-deep in water. For the most part, however, Roethlisberger held the offense together, and the score stood 3-0 at halftime.

The start of the second half was delayed so that the grounds crew could bring in more bags of dirt to dam the pooling water. Despite driving rain during the second half, Pittsburgh remained steady. The defense stopped Miami from getting a first down with a quarterback sneak on fourth and inches. In the resulting possession, Jeff Reed cleared a 51-yard field goal to bring the score to 6-0. In the fourth quarter, Miami managed to squeeze in a field goal. With 6:16 remaining, Pittsburgh's Hines Ward dove for a seven-yard touchdown catch. Jeff Reed's extra point was good. Still plagued by **turnovers**, the Dolphins had no answer for Pittsburgh. The Steelers held on for a slippery 13-3 victory in the worst conditions some of the players had ever experienced. The bad omens that opened the day turned out to be a grand opportunity for Roethlisberger. He successfully led the team through a rough game. His perseverance earned his teammates' respect. "He came out and did a tremendous job," Ward said about Roethlisberger. "He played his heart out."

After the game, Roethlisberger kept his composure, just as he had on the field, and seasoned it with a pinch of humor. "It's good to get that game out of the way," he said, as quoted by the Associated Press, "in case we ever play in a hurricane again—which I doubt we will."

Big Ben Emerges

When Ben Roethlisberger was at Miami of Ohio, he took a short drive to visit the Cincinnati Bengals' training camp. From a roped-off area, he watched quarterback Carson Palmer practice. At the time, he thought that the Bengals were working their No. 1 draft pick just the way they should be. Rather than throwing him right into the starting lineup, unprepared to deal with complicated NFL defenses, the Bengals allowed Palmer time to learn their offense and the league while veteran Jon Kitna played. The Pittsburgh Steelers had planned to ease Roethlisberger into the lineup in much the same way. For Pittsburgh, however, destiny had plans of its own.

In Game 4 of the 2004 season, Roethlisberger and Palmer faced off—a quarterback of careful design versus a rookie quarterback under the gun. It was a potentially pivotal game for both teams. The Bengals' finely tuned quarterback had had a less than spectacular start, going 30 possessions without a touchdown. In a 23-9 loss to Baltimore, Palmer had been sacked four times and threw three interceptions. The Bengals faced the possibility of going 1–3 into a **bye week**, the same record they had in 2003. In the previous season, Cincinnati made a comeback of sorts—at one point winning seven of nine games—but the Bengals still did not make the playoffs. The Bengals did not want to fall too far behind again this early in the season. Likewise, the Steelers were in the same spot a year ago. They were 2–1 when their season unraveled with five straight losses, which ultimately led to a 6–10 finish.

Palmer and Cincinnati started the dual in the first quarter with their second drive, which ended in a two-yard touchdown pass to Jeremi Johnson. Cincinnati had gotten the ball after a fumble by Pittsburgh's Duce Staley. The Steelers, though, quickly got their revenge on the next possession with a 55-yard drive and a two-yard touchdown run by Jerome Bettis. Roethlisberger's impressive five-play drive included a 30-yard completion to wide receiver Plaxico Burress. At the end of the first quarter, the game was tied 7-7. Early in the second quarter, Roethlisberger completed an 11-play, 80-yard drive with a touchdown pass to Verron Haynes. By halftime, all the Bengals could muster was a field goal, leaving the score 14-10 in favor of Pittsburgh.

At the start the second half, Palmer showed that he was not about to give up. On Cincinnati's opening drive, he moved the chains 71 yards for a touchdown to running back Rudi Johnson. The Bengals took the lead 17-14. With 5:28 to go in the third quarter, Pittsburgh tried to take advantage of a Cincinnati fumble but without luck. The Steelers were forced to punt. On their next possession, though, Roethlisberger led the Steelers offense 89 yards to a short touchdown run by Bettis. The 13-play drive, which ate up 6:32 and carried over into the fourth quarter, put

Pittsburgh back on top 21-17. Toward the end of the game, Steelers safety Troy Polamalu intercepted Palmer and returned the ball 26 yards for a touchdown. With only 2:19 remaining, Cincinnati was unable to answer, and Pittsburgh emerged victorious 28-17. Whether or not the win meant that heart won out over training, Roethlisberger was making a statement and people were taking notice.

Roethlisberger was 2–0 as a starter, and his team began to rally around him. Against the Bengals, he completed 17 of 25 passes for 174 yards, a touchdown, and no interceptions. In an Associated Press article, Plaxico Burress commented, "You can just see him coming into his own. He doesn't let anything bother him, and that's what I like about him." Although he was still a rookie making some mistakes, his teammates could do the math—he was certainly making more good plays than bad ones. "I have not mastered this offense by any means," Roethlisberger admitted after the Cincinnati game. "But the thing is we got the victory. You lead the team when they need it the most; you go down the field and score." Undoubtedly, Roethlisberger realized—as did the rest of his team—that he was only going to improve.

Some opponents, however, did not share the Steelers' optimism. In Week 5, Pittsburgh would face the Cleveland Browns. Before the matchup, Browns safety Earl Little said that Roethlisberger was not Cleveland's greatest worry. In his opinion, the Steelers were only asking the rookie to manage the offense in Maddox's absence and to avoid making costly mistakes. As it turned out, Little and the Browns drastically underestimated Roethlisberger's talent.

On October 10, Roethlisberger stumped Cleveland with his running moves and creativity. He completed 16 of 21 passes for 231 yards and one touchdown, and he scored on his own touchdown run. The opening drive was over in three quick and painful plays, with Staley running 25 yards up the middle to score a touchdown. For a moment, the Browns may have

With this dive across the goal line, Ben Roethlisberger scored the first rushing touchdown of his NFL career. The touchdown came in his third career start—in the first quarter of a game on October 10, 2004, against the Cleveland Browns. Pittsburgh beat their AFC North rivals 34-23.

thought that Roethlisberger had just gotten lucky. Indeed, on Pittsburgh's next possession, Roethlisberger threw an interception to Cleveland's Chris Crocker, who returned it for a 20-yard touchdown.

With the score tied 7-7, Roethlisberger scrambled to avoid defensive end Ebenezer Ekuban only to get hit by defender Orpheus Roye, but not before he found Burress for a 51-yard pass to the Cleveland 9. A three-yard **rush** by Staley put the ball at Cleveland's 6-yard line. Not the least bit rattled by Roye's hit, Roethlisberger powered a show-stopping run up the middle for his first NFL rushing touchdown. Now down 14-7, the Browns perhaps began to reconsider how big this new kid really was. Cleveland managed to put up a field goal before the end of the first quarter, bringing the Browns within four points. Roethlisberger, though, led the Steelers into field-goal range at the start of the second quarter. Kicker Jeff Reed split the uprights for a 47-yard field goal, putting Pittsburgh ahead by seven. On the Steelers' next possession, Roethlisberger show-cased his running threat. He rolled out of the pocket, freezing the defense for a moment while Burress slipped five yards behind Browns cornerback Anthony Henry. Roethlisberger connected with Burress for an unguarded 37-yard touchdown pass. The extra point was good, and Pittsburgh led 24-10. Once again, the best Cleveland could muster was another field goal. Before the end of the first half, though, Pittsburgh neatly erased it with a field goal of its own.

At the start of the second half, Roethlisberger and the Steelers held a 14-point lead over Cleveland. On the first possession, Roethlisberger moved the chains from Pittsburgh's 37-yard line—63 yards—ending the drive with Jerome Bettis's three-yard rushing touchdown. Pittsburgh was now up 34-13. Cleveland held Roethlisberger scoreless for the rest of the game and added a field goal and a touchdown, but it was not enough to catch the Steelers. Pittsburgh walked away with a 34-23 victory. The Browns dropped two games behind Pittsburgh in the AFC North.

For Roethlisberger, the game was all starting to come together. His jaw-dropping throws and natural athleticism were proof that Big Ben was a force in his own right. Those who underestimated his role in Pittsburgh were entertaining second thoughts. "He played like a veteran," Roye, the Browns' defensive tackle, said after the game in an Associated Press article. "You couldn't tell he was a rookie." The heavily publicized Eli Manning and Philip Rivers were sitting on the bench, while Roethlisberger became only the sixth rookie quarterback to win his first three starts since 1970. Pittsburgh's record was 4–1 for only the third time in 22 seasons. Showing the poise of a veteran, Roethlisberger remained humble. He gave credit to his teammates. "A lot of those plays aren't called, but the linemen are doing a great job of blocking and the wide receivers are getting open," Roethlisberger said. "For me it's easy—all I've got to do is run and throw the football." Complementing Roethlisberger, Staley had muscled three consecutive 100-yard rushing games, and against Cleveland, Burress pulled down six catches for 136 yards.

ANOTHER MARINO?

The week before the Cowboys would face the Steelers, a reporter asked Dallas coach Bill Parcells to name the last rookie quarterback who impressed him as much as Roethlisberger. Parcells admitted that Roethlisberger was the best quarterback prospect he had seen in years. In fact, he hadn't seen anyone come into the league like Roethlisberger since Dan Marino, the Dolphins' star who debuted in 1983.

The Roethlisberger-Marino comparison was one that most Steelers fans could appreciate. After their Super Bowl successes of the 1970s, the Steelers took a downward slide. Pittsburgh regretted not drafting Marino—who grew up in the Steel City and played at the University of Pittsburgh—as its quarterback in 1983. Partly because of this decision, the team never found a comparable replacement for Hall of Fame quarterback Terry Bradshaw. From 1980 to 1993, Pittsburgh won only two playoff games. Parcells now suggested that perhaps Pittsburgh had finally found its Marino. "I am very, very impressed," Parcells told the Associated Press, "and it's not just because he is an opponent."

While Roethlisberger graciously accepted the praise, he remained cautious. Coming less than a week before the game,

Dallas Cowboys coach Bill Parcells said that Ben Roethlisberger was the best quarterback prospect he had seen since Dan Marino of the Miami Dolphins came into the league in 1983. Marino, too, saw shades of himself in the young Pittsburgh player. Here, Roethlisberger and Marino met to tape an interview in November 2004.

Parcells's compliments could also be seen as a bit of pregame psychological trickery from a veteran coach. Roethlisberger did not want to let Parcells get into his head. He just wanted to go out and play his game—and win. In response, Roethlisberger also said that any comparisons to Marino should wait for another 15 years or so. During his 17-season NFL career, Marino threw for 61,361 yards. At the time, this was nearly 10,000 more yards than any other quarterback in league history. (In 2007, Green Bay quarterback Brett Favre broke Marino's record.) Roethlisberger kept his ego in check. He had only played three games. He knew it was too early to be making those kinds of statements. "If I can be half as good as Marino, I'll be incredibly happy,"

ASK MARINO

During Ben Roethlisberger's rookie year, a lot of insiders around the NFL compared him to Dan Marino. Although flattered, Big Ben downplayed the comments. "It's a little too early to be putting those statements on it," he said in *Roethlisberger: Pittsburgh's Own Big Ben*. However, someone other than the coaches and the players was spotting similarities—Dan Marino was, too.

"A lot of the things he does kind of remind me of some of the things I was able to do when I played," Marino said in an Associated Press article. Impressed by Roethlisberger's awareness in the pocket and his ability to move while still making throws downfield, Marino said, "You can't teach those kinds of instincts, and that's something he has going for him that a lot of the guys in the league don't have."

When Marino took over for the benched David Woodley during his rookie season with the Miami Dolphins in 1983, he looked and felt just as comfortable as Roethlisberger did. When Marino was asked how long it took a player to know he could play, he said, "I think you realize pretty quick. . . . Because you compare yourself to other people and what they've done." In his rookie season, Marino was 173 of 296 for 2,210 yards, 20 touchdowns, and six interceptions in 11 games. At the end of the 2004 season, Roethlisberger had completed 196 of 295 passes for 2,621 yards, with 17 touchdowns and 11 interceptions in 14 games. "He's not turning the ball over . . . and that's more important than percentage," Marino said. "That's the biggest thing a quarterback has to deal with and worry about."

Perhaps many people discounted the comparisons of a young rookie quarterback to the great Dan Marino. Few could argue, however, when they asked Marino, and he agreed.

Roethlisberger said, as quoted in *Roethlisberger: Pittsburgh's Own Big Ben*. He was, however, having a better start than Bradshaw, who in his first year completed only six touchdown passes and had 24 interceptions. On October 17, Roethlisberger would try to do what no Steelers quarterback had accomplished since Bradshaw—a win in Dallas.

Roethlisberger proved sharp from the beginning of the game. When the Cowboys scored on a 21-yard touchdown run on their opening drive, he marched the offense downfield to tie the game with an amazing five-yard pass to Burress. In this one play, Roethlisberger showed more mobility than Marino ever did. He scrambled out of the pocket to his right, then fired the ball to Burress an instant before defender Marcellus Wiley flattened him from behind. The play triggered a frenzy from the many Steelers fans in the stands. For a minute—with thousands of "Terrible Towels" spinning frantically—Texas Stadium looked more like a Pittsburgh home game.

In the third quarter, Dallas quarterback Vinny Testaverde connected with Keyshawn Johnson on a 22-yard touchdown, giving the Cowboys a 20-10 lead. The Steelers, however, made it 20-17 when Roethlisberger—standing flat-footed in the pocket—rifled a pass to the back of the end zone into the hands of tight end Jerame Tuman. With less than three minutes left in the game, Dallas still held the lead, with possession on the Steelers' 47-yard line. Facing third down, Testaverde dropped back to pass. The Pittsburgh defense blitzed. Steelers linebacker James Farrior, who already had two sacks and caused two fumbles, plowed through the line to knock the ball loose again. Defensive tackle Kimo von Oelhoffen picked it up and ran to the Dallas 24-yard line. Roethlisberger took over and drove the ball down to the 2-yard line. Bettis thundered into the end zone for the final touchdown in the last minute.

Dallas, though, had one last chance at victory. The Cowboys covered 30 yards on a pass and **lateral** that moved

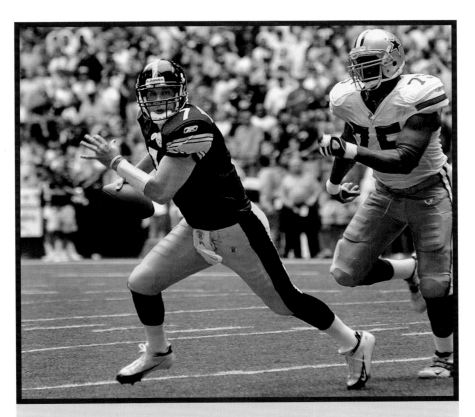

Pursued by Dallas defensive end Marcellus Wiley, Ben Roethlisberger scrambled out of the pocket during a game on October 17, 2004. Just before Wiley hit him, Roethlisberger fired off a five-yard touchdown pass to Plaxico Burress for Pittsburgh's first score of the game.

the ball to the Pittsburgh 30-yard line with one second left on the clock. Testaverde's final throw into the end zone, though, fell incomplete.

Dallas's untimely fumble was a definite gift for the Steelers, but the win was far from easy. All day, Roethlisberger stood in the pocket and made tough throws against a rugged pass rush. Although he was sacked three times, his quick moves helped him avoided several others. He completed 21 of 25 passes for two touchdowns, completing nine straight throws on the Steelers' last two scoring drives and 11 straight throws in one stretch. "He can flat-out play," Burress said, as quoted by the Associated Press. "I think Parcells was right."

Pittsburgh's 24-20 win over Dallas certainly wooed players, fans, and the press. But Big Ben still had a lot to prove. Next, after the Steelers' bye week, he would face the undefeated New England Patriots. Few believed that he could handle the Patriots' complex defense or the pressure of playing against a team that had won an NFL-record 21 straight games, going back to the 2003 season.

Best Rookie Ever?

Pittsburgh's success in 2004 was not totally linked to rookie Ben Roethlisberger. The Steelers' running game—the NFL's second-worst in 2003—once again ranked in the upper quarter of the league, thanks to the addition of Duce Staley, who already had three consecutive 100-yard games. Also, the defense had improved under new defensive coordinator Dick LeBeau, who brought back pressure and blitzing. One of those blitzes led to the fumble by Dallas's Vinny Testaverde and Pittsburgh's resulting win. It was the fifteenth forced turnover of the season, only 10 fewer than the Steelers had forced in all 16 games of the 2003 season. Still, Roethlisberger's effect on the team was immediate and dramatic. In 2003, Pittsburgh lost five times by a touchdown or less. Under Roethlisberger, the team rallied two times for fourth-quarter wins. He was bringing back confidence. His teammates had confidence in one another, and they believed they could find a way to win.

Until this point, however, Pittsburgh had benefited from a favorable schedule. Their one loss was to the only team with a winning record—Baltimore. The final 10 weeks would be tougher. At this point in the season, two teams remained unbeaten—the defending Super Bowl champion Patriots and the Eagles—and the Steelers had to face them both in the next two weeks. Would the rookie getting all the hype be able to stand up to the toughest teams?

Going into Week 8, Roethlisberger ranked fourth in passer rating, after far more experienced quarterbacks Daunte Culpepper, Peyton Manning, and Donovan McNabb. His 69 percent completion rate was exceptional for any quarterback, especially one who was not supposed to be on the field yet. His abilities would be put to the test in playing undefeated teams back-to-back.

On Halloween night at Heinz Field in Pittsburgh, the Patriots started the game off like any other—scoring with a field goal, the fifteenth-straight game in which the Patriots scored first. After that, it seemed as if all the treats were for the Steelers. Midway through the first quarter, Patriot Pro Bowler Ty Law was sidelined with an injured left foot. On the next play, Roethlisberger threw a flawless 47-yard pass to Plaxico Burress, who burned past Law's replacement—Randall Gay—for a touchdown. On the first play of the Patriots' next possession, Super Bowl-winning quarterback Tom Brady fumbled after a hard hit from Steelers linebacker Joey Porter. Pittsburgh recovered the fumble, and Roethlisberger capitalized on it—ending with a four-yard touchdown pass to Burress. Pittsburgh scored quickly again, with Deshea Townsend returning an interception 39 yards for a touchdown. At the end of the first quarter, the Steelers were cruising 21-3. By halftime, it was 24-10, Pittsburgh.

Roethlisberger, though, was not celebrating yet. Usually, Brady plays his best during the second half. This night, though,

Ben Roethlisberger and Plaxico Burress celebrated the first of their two first-quarter touchdown passes in the Steelers' October 31, 2004, game against the New England Patriots. Roethlisberger and the Steelers ended the Patriots' 21-game winning streak with a decisive 34-20 victory.

belonged to Pittsburgh. On the first drive of the second half, Patriots running back Kevin Faulk fumbled, and Pittsburgh turned it into another touchdown. Less than two minutes into the second half, the Steelers had mounted a monstrous 31-10 lead. Later in the third quarter, Brady led the Patriots on an 11-play, 59-yard drive, but the Pittsburgh defense held them to a field goal. Then, Roethlisberger brought the offense back down the field for a Pittsburgh field goal. With about six-and-a-half minutes remaining, Brady hit David Givens for a touchdown, but it was too little, too late. The Steelers racked up a dominant 34-20 victory, ending the Patriots' 21-game winning streak.

Pittsburgh was the first team to beat the Patriots since Washington slipped past them 20-17 on September 28, 2003. Now, the so-called team to beat shared a 6–1 record with the Steelers. The sports experts who predicted that Roethlisberger had no chance to beat the Patriots' defense were stunned. "They're finding out around the league," Burress told the Associated Press. Next up, Pittsburgh would face the NFL's only remaining unbeaten team—Philadelphia (7–0). Everyone seemed to be pondering the same question. Could Roethlisberger take out two top teams in back-to-back games? His completion percentage had risen to 70.1 percent, and he had a 104.7 passer rating, with nine touchdowns, four interceptions, and only one interception in his last 116 passes. Roethlisberger tried to keep a level head and stay focused. "We keep saying it over and over again: Let's not get too excited," Roethlisberger said, as quoted in an article on ESPN.com. Not every Steeler held back, though. "We're a hard team to beat," wide receiver Hines Ward said.

PERFECT 10

Playing unbeaten teams one after the other in midseason or beyond is a rare occurrence. The last time the NFL witnessed it was when the Detroit Lions lost twice to the undefeated Chicago Bears in 1934 to close out the season. When it came to the Pittsburgh Steelers, ears were perking up around the country. Thanks in large part to the 22-year-old Roethlisberger, the Steelers were off to their best seven-game start in Bill Cowher's 13 seasons as a coach. Roethlisberger was far from finished, however. Cowher already made it clear that, even though Tommy Maddox was ready to play again, Big Ben would still be his starter.

Cowher's decision proved to be a smart one. If sports fans thought that Pittsburgh devastated New England, then the Steelers totally annihilated Philadelphia. On the first three possessions, Roethlisberger's offense tore open a 21-0 lead. Hines Ward scored on the first two drives—on a 16-yard **reverse** and a 20-yard reception. Roethlisberger also had help from Bettis's 149 yards of rushing, his fifty-fifth career 100-yard game. The previous week, Pittsburgh had outrushed New England 221 yards to 5 yards. In Week 9, the Steelers outran the Eagles 252 to 23 and outgained them 420 to 111. Pittsburgh's defense turned up the heat, holding quarterback Donovan McNabb to 15 of 24 for 109 yards, with no touchdowns and an interception. Roethlisberger was 11 of 18 for 183 yards, two touchdowns, and one interception. The result was a crushing 27-3 victory and an end to the Eagles' seven-game winning streak. Pittsburgh had made sure that there was no one undefeated in the NFL—that is, of course, except Ben Roethlisberger.

Roethlisberger continued to excel over the next three weeks, with wins against Cleveland (24-10), Cincinnati (19-14), and Washington (16-7). Week 13 took Pittsburgh on the road to Alltel Stadium in Jacksonville, Florida, for a prime-time Sunday night game. Once again, Roethlisberger handled the pressure with the poise of a veteran. His first touchdown completed a seven-play, 77-yard drive, as he nailed Ward for a 37-yard score. Jacksonville's quarterback Byron Leftwich countered with a 12-play, 73-yard drive, hitting Troy Edwards for a 22-yard touchdown. Pittsburgh broke the tie when Roethlisberger completed a 26-yard pass to tight end Jay Riemersma. By the end of the third quarter, the Jaguars had tacked on two field goals, bringing them within one point, 14-13.

With 1:55 left in the game, Jacksonville's kicker Josh Scobee cleared a 36-yard field goal to put the Jaguars ahead 16-14. On the ensuing drive, Roethlisberger went 3 of 4 for 39 yards to set up a 37-yard field goal for Jeff Reed. His only incompletion was a spike after he calmly let the clock run down, leaving the Jaguars with little time for a comeback. Reed made the game-winning field goal with 18 seconds to play. Jacksonville had one last shot at a win after a 19-yard completion from

THE CHIN

Former Steelers coach Bill Cowher has a strange yet appropriate nickname—"The Chin." Anyone who has witnessed him scowling on the sideline, his iron-set jaw jutting out, knows exactly where it comes from. "Everyone thinks he's tough—he is—but he's a players' coach," Steelers receiver Hines Ward said about him in *Tough as Steel*. "His door is always open if you have a problem, or just want to talk. Yes, he gets angry, but most of the time, he's right."

Cowher practically bleeds Pittsburgh. He was born and raised in Crafton, Pennsylvania, a suburb of Pittsburgh, and settled behind the Steel Curtain for a 15-season run as coach in one of the NFL's proudest football towns. He started his NFL career as a free-agent linebacker with the Philadelphia Eagles in 1979. He spent his next three seasons with the Cleveland Browns. In 1983, he was traded back to the Eagles, where he played two more years. In 1985 at 28, Cowher began his coaching career with the Browns, first as a special-teams coach in 1985 and 1986. Then, he served as a **secondary** coach in 1987 and 1988 before going to Kansas City as a defensive coordinator in 1989.

On January 21, 1992, Cowher replaced Chuck Noll as the fifteenth head coach in Steelers history. Although Cowher was young for a head coach—34 years old, then the youngest coach in the league, Steelers chairman Dan Rooney believed in his decision. "I could see in him a guy who would have success over the long haul," Rooney said in *Tough as Steel*. "His roots have

Leftwich to Jimmy Smith, which left Scobee a 60-yard field-goal attempt. The kick, though, fell just short and wide right. Roethlisberger had achieved his first last-minute, game-winning drive of his career. Finishing the night at 14 of 17 for 221 yards,

helped him. He knows Pittsburgh, he understands the people, and he thinks of it as home."

Under Cowher, the team showed immediate improvement from a disappointing 7–9 season in 1991. In 1992, Pittsburgh went 11–5 and earned home-field advantage in the AFC playoffs. After missing the playoffs six out of the previous seven years, it was just the rush the Steelers—and their fans—needed. And just as Rooney predicted, Cowher brought success over the years. In 1995, at age 38, Cowher became the youngest coach to lead his team to a Super Bowl. The Steelers, though, fell to Dallas 27-17. He was only the second coach in NFL history to lead his team to the playoffs in each of his first six seasons. Over the course of 15 seasons, Pittsburgh captured eight division titles, earned 10 playoff berths, played in 21 playoff games, advanced to six AFC Championship Games, and made two Super Bowl appearances—winning one. Cowher is one of only six NFL coaches to claim at least seven division titles. At the end of 2005, the Steelers had the best record of any team in the NFL since Cowher had been hired as head coach.

After announcing his retirement in January 2007, Cowher was replaced by Mike Tomlin, who had been the defensive coordinator of the Minnesota Vikings. Cowher still could not get football out of his blood, though. In February 2007, he joined James Brown, Dan Marino, Shannon Sharpe, and Boomer Esiason on *The NFL Today* on CBS as a studio analyst.

Steelers head coach Bill Cowher joked with Ben Roethlisberger in the fourth quarter of Pittsburgh's 27-3 win over Philadelphia on November 7, 2004. With their wins over New England and Philadelphia, the Steelers had defeated two unbeaten teams in back-to-back games.

two touchdowns, and a passer rating of 158 (just three-tenths of a point from perfection), Roethlisberger had a perfect-10 winning streak. He even rushed for 40 yards. Now the Steelers were one game away from clinching the AFC North, and they also held the tiebreaker for home-field advantage in the AFC over the New England Patriots.

A FAN FAVORITE

These were confidence-boosting times for Roethlisberger, as a rookie quarterback in the midst of an eye-catching winning streak. He was the talk of the NFL, and in Pittsburgh, he was the newest sensation among sports fans, instantly recognizable whenever he appeared in public. Just a few games into his career, and he had already changed some of his off-field routines—now he would run all his errands in one shot early in the week, checking off items from a lengthy to-do list.

Still, as an article in *Sports Illustrated* described, a trip to a local mall could cause a stir, with fans wanting Roethlisberger's autograph or a picture with him. One fan bought a football and a Sharpie after spotting Roethlisberger at the mall. In getting the autograph, the fan accidentally got an ink stain on Roethlisberger's hoodie. No sweat, to Ben. "Hey, as long as the guy is happy," he said. "If the fans are happy, I'm happy."

Roethlisberger jerseys were flying off the shelves, and also popular was the Roethlisburger—a hoagie sandwich sold at Peppi's. The sub, with beef, sausage, scrambled eggs, and American cheese, sold for $7—matching his jersey number.

Still, he remained grounded. For instance, Roethlisberger probably had the choice of any table at any of the upscale establishments along Pittsburgh's Strip. On most Monday nights, though, he and a few friends could be found at Jack's, a nondescript bar on the city's South Side. His family, too, was there for Roethlisberger. He lived by himself in a townhouse a few miles from the Steelers' practice complex. For home games, Ken and Brenda Roethlisberger stayed with Ben in Pittsburgh. "I have a great family," Roethlisberger said. "I can call them and they don't want to talk just football. They want to find out how my day went outside of football. . . . It is so key for me to have that comfort blanket back home."

TO THE PLAYOFFS

After another victory against the New York Jets, which clinched the AFC North title for the Steelers, Roethlisberger was set to meet his draft-day rival, Eli Manning, who was now starting for the New York Giants. Saturday, December 18, brought the much-anticipated matchup between Roethlisberger and Manning. Until that game, Manning had struggled, losing his first four starts. The Giants, though, were about to turn around their prospects.

Giants receiver Willie Ponder returned the opening kickoff 91 yards for a touchdown. It was the first kickoff return for a touchdown in a home game in the entire 80-year history of the Giants. Two possessions later, Pittsburgh tied it up 7-7 when Roethlisberger made a lateral pass to Antwaan Randle El. Randle El then threw a 10-yard shovel pass across the middle to Verron Haynes for the touchdown. Manning had an answer for that glitzy play, though—a 55-yard drive that ended with a two-yard touchdown pass to Jeremy Shockey. The Giants took the lead 14-7. Pittsburgh tried to tie the game again but had to settle for a field goal.

The second quarter belonged to the Steelers. Roethlisberger found Randle El for a 35-yard touchdown to put Pittsburgh ahead 17-14. Then, near the end of the half, Jeff Reed cleared a 21-yard field goal to push the lead to 20-14. In the third quarter, a Giants field goal was quickly matched by Pittsburgh, changing the score to 23-17 in favor of Pittsburgh. On the next possession, Manning fired across the middle to Marcellus Rivers for a short one-yard touchdown, giving New York a 24-23 lead.

In the beginning of the fourth quarter, Roethlisberger moved the chains 60 yards to the Giants' 10-yard line, but the Steelers were forced to settle for a field goal. The score, however, gave them a brief lead. Then, Manning hit Amani Toomer for back-to-back 17-yard passes and found Ike Hilliard for a 15-yard pass to the Pittsburgh 1-yard line. The 51-yard drive set up a go-ahead touchdown run for the Giants' Tiki Barber, pulling New York ahead 30-26. Manning tried for a two-point conversion but was sacked. The game was far from over, though. On the Steelers' next possession, Roethlisberger drove the offense from Pittsburgh's 33 to the Giants' 8-yard line, setting up a touchdown run by Bettis. The 67-yard drive included nine-yard and 11-yard passes to Ward and a 36-yarder to Randle El. With 4:57 left on the clock, the Steelers had regained the lead, 33-30. Unable to make a comeback, Manning had to bow to Roethlisberger, and Pittsburgh captured its twelfth straight win.

That afternoon, Roethlisberger threw for a season-high 316 yards. What stood out as the difference between Manning and Roethlisberger was that Big Ben could make his biggest plays when the game was on the line. "In the fourth quarter, he has a feel for the game and an understanding of the game and he manages it well," coach Bill Cowher said in an article on ESPN.com. Roethlisberger, who had not lost in 25 straight starts from college into the pros, just kept focusing on winning the next game. "I don't want to ever remember what it's like to lose," he said.

Roethlisberger's memory wouldn't need to be jogged yet in Week 16 against the Baltimore Ravens, either. As the only team to beat Pittsburgh all season, perhaps the Ravens thought they had an edge. Baltimore managed to keep up until the third quarter. Then, working a run-heavy offense, Roethlisberger threw his second touchdown pass—a two-yarder to Jerame Tuman. A split second later, Ravens defender Terrell Suggs pounded Roethlisberger from the **blind side**. Suggs's **roughing-the-passer** penalty paled in comparison to what Pittsburgh fans watched from their seats at Heinz Field— Roethlisberger was injured. With a clump of grass wedged in the left side of his face mask, Roethlisberger limped off the field. Although he wore a protective jacket under his uniform, as many NFL quarterbacks do, he had taken a serious blow to the ribs. On Pittsburgh's next drive, though, he was back in the game. He completed a 26-yard pass to Burress and a nine-yarder to Bettis before the end of the third quarter, but he winced every time he threw. Cowher did not want to take a chance of hurting Roethlisberger more. In the fourth quarter, Tommy Maddox took over, driving for a field goal to secure a 20-7 win over Baltimore.

Everyone in Pittsburgh—which fans now referred to as Roethlisburgh—wondered how seriously Big Ben was hurt.

A blind-side hit from Baltimore's Terrell Suggs injured Ben Roethlisberger in the third quarter of a game on December 26, 2004. Roethlisberger played a few more downs before coach Bill Cowher pulled him from the rest of the game. Roethlisberger also sat out the final game of the regular season to rest up for Pittsburgh's playoff run.

The Steelers' 14–1 record had secured a first-round bye and home-field advantage throughout the AFC playoffs. Would the rookie quarterback who led them there be able to play? Cowher quickly calmed the worst fears of Steelers fans. Roethlisberger would not play in the final regular-season game at Buffalo, but he would be back for the playoffs. In Buffalo, Maddox—the veteran turned backup—would lead the Pittsburgh offense in Roethlisberger's absence. On January 2,

2005, at Ralph Wilson Stadium, Maddox kept the winning record rolling with a 29-24 victory over the Bills. Meanwhile, Roethlisberger had two more weeks to heal before heading into the divisional playoff game. In the **wild-card** games during the first week of the playoffs, the New York Jets beat San Diego, 20-17, and the Indianapolis Colts defeated the Denver Broncos, 49-24. The Steelers' opponent in their first playoff game, on January 15, would be the Jets.

The Steelers started off strong in what would turn out to be a wild overtime playoff game. Jeff Reed gave the Steelers the first score of the day with a 45-yard field goal. Pittsburgh quickly got the ball back after Troy Polamalu intercepted a pass by Jets quarterback Chad Pennington. Five plays and 25 yards later, Bettis rumbled into the end zone for a three-yard touchdown, giving the Steelers a 10-0 lead. Jets kicker Doug Brien started the second-quarter scoring with a 42-yard field goal. Then, New York receiver Santana Moss scored on 75-yard punt return, the first punt return for a touchdown in Jets playoff history. The return—which tied the game 10-10—was a jolt to the Steelers' usually strong **special teams**, which had allowed only one punt return longer than 10 yards in the previous 11 games.

In the second half, Pittsburgh seemed to be jinxed. Two huge turnovers looked to have cost the Steelers the game. In the third quarter, a Roethlisberger pass was intercepted by Reggie Tongue and returned for an 86-yard touchdown that put the Jets ahead 17-10. Then, early in the fourth, Bettis fumbled at the Jets' 24-yard line, his first fumble in 353 carries or receptions all season. At this point, though, luck seemed to switch sides. Roethlisberger led a pivotal scoring drive, ending with a four-yard flip to Hines Ward. The score was tied at 17. The Jets, though, looked as if they might pull ahead on their next drive. All Brien had to do was clear a 47-yard field goal. Roethlisberger watched in suspense from the sidelines. The ball hit the goal post. It was no good. The Steelers had another chance. They took over the ball with two minutes remaining.

On the first play, though, Roethlisberger was intercepted by Jets cornerback David Barrett. It was the kind of mistake a rookie quarterback might make in the playoffs, but the kind Roethlisberger had rarely made during his 13–0 season. The Jets drove from Pittsburgh's 37 to the 25, with 4 seconds left, giving Brien a chance at a 43-yard field goal and some redemption. From the Steelers' sidelines, it seemed certain that their greatest season since the 1970s was all but lost, Roethlisberger's unbeaten rookie season over. But to everyone's astonishment, the kick sailed wide left—not even close. The game went into overtime. The Jets got the ball first but had to punt. On Pittsburgh's first possession, Roethlisberger moved the chains 72 yards in 14 plays to the Jets' 15-yard line, setting up a 33-yard field-goal attempt. Reed did what Brien could not do—twice—make the game-winning field goal. Pittsburgh won in overtime, 20-17.

Undoubtedly, Roethlisberger was grateful for Brien's all-out miracle misses. The win, though, was not enough to satisfy him. "I did everything I could to lose the game," Roethlisberger said in an article on ESPN.com. "I've got to play better. That was terrible. The game we played today is not going to cut it." Roethlisberger went into the game the same way he had all regular season—calm and relaxed. If he planned to win the AFC Championship against the Patriots, he would have to do something differently. "Maybe next week I need to be a little more stressed," he said.

On January 23, Roethlisberger learned that paybacks can be rough. At 11°F (-12°C), the game was the second-coldest in Steeler history. But the stiff wind didn't turn nearly as cold as Pittsburgh's fans, who went from feverishly twirling their Terrible Towels to booing their beloved Big Ben. Tom Brady gave Roethlisberger a lesson in quarterbacking a championship game. As Roethlisberger later commented, "They threw the book at us." Big Ben was intercepted on his first pass, which led to a 48-yard field goal by Adam Vinatieri. On Pittsburgh's next possession, Bettis fumbled. Once again, Brady took advantage of the turnover, hooking up with Deion Branch for a 60-yard touchdown on the very next play. The Steelers managed to sneak in a field goal before the end of the first quarter, but the Patriots held a 10-3 lead. In the second quarter, Brady added another touchdown. Then, Pittsburgh showed some signs of life. Roethlisberger drove the offense 58 yards to the Patriots' 19-yard line. But on second down, he underthrew Tuman, and the pass was intercepted by New England safety Rodney Harrison. Harrison returned it 87 yards for a touchdown, giving the Patriots a 24-3 halftime lead.

During the second half, Roethlisberger managed to get the offense going, but the Steelers could not catch up. The Patriots seemed to answer almost every score. Roethlisberger opened the third quarter with a touchdown, but Brady followed it with a 69-yard touchdown drive. Before the end of the third quarter, Roethlisberger completed a 30-yard touchdown pass to Ward, closing the margin to 31-17. In the fourth quarter, Pittsburgh came as close it would to New England with a field goal. Then, the Patriots led another field-goal-ending drive to boost the score to 34-20. Once again, Roethlisberger threw a costly interception, which resulted in another Patriot touchdown—the fifth touchdown of the day. With less than a minute to go, Roethlisberger managed to hit Burress for a seven-yard touchdown, which made the loss a little more respectable at 41-27.

Roethlisberger's amazing rookie season came to a deflating end. The loss was tough on him, but it was probably tougher on some of the other players. "It wasn't a great game on my part, but I learned an awful lot this season," Roethlisberger said. "We had a great season, but there are a lot of people— some in that locker room—that now think" the season was a disappointment. It *had* been a great season for a rookie quarterback, as Roethlisberger finished fifth in NFL passer rating with 98.1, beating Dan Marino's rookie rating of 96. He also

A dejected Ben Roethlisberger walked off the field during the waning seconds of Pittsburgh's defeat in the AFC Championship Game on January 23, 2005. The Patriots beat the Steelers 41-27, ending Roethlisberger's spectacular rookie season.

broke Marino's record for rookie completion percentage (66.4 percent). Roethlisberger became the first quarterback in NFL history to compile a 13–0 record during the regular season. He was named the Associated Press NFL Offensive Rookie of the Year and the *Sporting News* Rookie of the Year. In October, he was selected the AFC Offensive Rookie of the Month. In addition, he was honored with the 2004 Joe Greene Award, given to the Steelers' rookie of the year and voted on by the Pittsburgh Chapter of the Pro Football Writers of America. Although he never got too excited about his success, Ben Roethlisberger had delivered an incredible season—as one of the best rookie quarterbacks ever.

"One More Year"

A soft September sun fell on Heinz Field for the 2005 season opener. With the temperature climbing to a pleasant 75°F (24°C) by kickoff, it was the perfect day for football. Ben Roethlisberger's arm was as spectacular as the pale blue sky above him. Despite talk about a "Sophomore Jinx"—about being unable to repeat his fantastic rookie season—Roethlisberger walked off the field with a perfect 158.3 passer rating. He completed 9 of 11 passes for 218 yards and two touchdowns in a 34-7 win over the Tennessee Titans.

As usual, Roethlisberger showed his humility and gave credit to his teammates. "When you only throw a couple of balls, it's not hard to (have a perfect rating)," he said in *Tough as Steel*. "You get the ball close to our receivers, and they are going to make plays." He had a lot of help from tailback Willie Parker,

62

who mirrored Roethlisberger's perfection. In his first career start, Parker blasted past the Titans for 161 yards on 22 carries (7.3 yards per carry), including an 11-yard touchdown. He also ran a **screen pass** 48 yards for a total of 209 yards from the line of scrimmage. Like Roethlisberger the year before, Parker entered training camp a few slots down on the depth chart, behind Jerome Bettis, Duce Staley, and Verron Haynes. Injuries to Bettis and Staley, though, gave Parker the chance to play.

In the first quarter, the Titans easily drove 61 yards in 11 plays behind quarterback Steve McNair and running back Chris Brown. Tight end Ben Troupe capped off the drive with a one-yard touchdown reception. The Titans, however, failed to produce an encore, and Pittsburgh took over the Tennessee Waltz from that point. The Steelers scored on their first six possessions, four times in the first half, without a single turnover. On the other end, Tennessee dished out four turnovers—two fumbles and two interceptions—two that led to scores.

On the Steelers' first drive, Roethlisberger went 5 of 5 for 88 yards. His final pass sailed to rookie tight end Heath Miller for a touchdown. Jeff Reed tacked on two first-half field goals—both on turnovers. The first came after linebacker James Farrior forced a fumble, and the second score was thanks to an interception by Troy Polamalu. With 8:49 left in the first half, Roethlisberger connected with Antwaan Randle El for a 63-yard touchdown pass. On the opening drive of the second half, Roethlisberger hit Randle El with a 26-yard pass and Cedrick Wilson with a 14-yarder. The drive ended with an 11-yard scoring run from Parker, who had to bounce off two Tennessee defenders on his way to the end zone. Verron Haynes topped off the score with a five-yard touchdown run in the third quarter, which had been set up by a 45-yard burst by Parker.

The win was a great beginning to a promising year. And Roethlisberger had a big promise to keep. Last season, standing on the sidelines of the AFC Championship Game,

Keith Bulluck of the Tennessee Titans pressured Ben Roethlisberger during the season opener on September 11, 2005. Pittsburgh and Roethlisberger got off to an impressive start, as the Steelers won 34-7. Roethlisberger completed 9 of 11 passes for 218 yards, and he had a perfect 158.3 passer rating.

watching the clock tick down and knowing that the Steelers had lost, Roethlisberger turned to Bettis. Bettis had clocked 12 NFL seasons and was ready to hang it up. But Bettis, the fifth all-time rusher in NFL history, had yet to earn a Super Bowl ring. With tears welling in his eyes, Roethlisberger said, "Come back. I'll get you to the Super Bowl. Give me one more year." Those were some pretty powerful words, but they were enough to bring Bettis back. With its first win, Pittsburgh was on its way.

Pittsburgh delivered another thrashing in Week 2 in Houston, Texas. Roethlisberger did not need the sweltering heat to prove he was hot, pulling out another nearly perfect game.

He completed 14 of 21 passes for 254 yards, two touchdowns, and a 139.8 passer rating. Both the offense and the defense were cruising like a well-greased engine, with the fleet-footed Parker running 111 yards on 25 carries and a score for his second-consecutive 100-yard game and Polamalu leading the defense with three of Pittsburgh's eight sacks.

The Steelers wasted little time amassing a Texas-sized lead. On the opening series, Roethlisberger and Parker combined forces for 60 yards before Reed kicked a 37-yard field goal. A bumbling Texans offense fumbled on its first possession, and in just two plays, Roethlisberger found Hines Ward for a touchdown. Next possession, Roethlisberger led a nine-play, 92-yard drive in which he completed 5 of 6 passes for 98 total yards; the final play was a 14-yard touchdown pass to Ward. Before the half, Reed added another field goal, wilting Texas with a 20-0 lead.

Houston opened the third quarter with a touchdown, but Roethlisberger remained in command. On the next possession, on third and 5 from the Steelers' 37, Roethlisberger appeared trapped. Then he shuffled to his right, pumped, and fired the ball downfield to wide receiver Cedrick Wilson, who snatched it from the air for a 40-yard reception. Three plays later, Parker sealed the drive with a 10-yard touchdown. The Steelers roped a 27-7 victory over the Texans.

But all good things must come to an end, and for Roethlisberger, it happened in Week 3 against his nemesis Tom Brady. The Steelers versus the Patriots—the event had been "all the buzz" in the sports community since Week 1. For much of the game, the two teams went back and forth. Patriots running back Corey Dillon opened the scoring in the first quarter with a four-yard touchdown. Next, the Steelers tied the game when Roethlisberger hit Ward for an 85-yard touchdown reception. Reed added a 33-yard first-quarter field goal to give Pittsburgh a 10-7 lead. The two teams played a scoreless second quarter.

In the third quarter, Reed tacked on a second field goal for a 13-7 edge, but the Patriots counterattacked. Two field goals by Adam Vinatieri sandwiched a touchdown run by Dillon to make the score 20-13 with 3:19 remaining. Roethlisberger led an efficient late-game drive that ended with a four-yard pass to Ward for the game-tying touchdown. With 1:21 left in the game, Brady calmly engineered a final 37-yard drive, completing 3 of 3, to set up Vinatieri's game-winning 43-yard field goal with one second remaining. The 23-20 loss brought an end to Roethlisberger's NFL record of 15 consecutive regular-season victories as a starter.

On October 10, a Monday night, the Steelers and the Chargers put on the game of the year at Qualcomm Stadium in San Diego. The Chargers entered the game with one of the league's most lethal offenses, having scored 86 points in the previous two games. The Steelers' defense, however, stifled them early—holding San Diego to just one first down in the first quarter. Still, Pittsburgh's offense had little to show in return, as it failed to nail a first down in its first two possessions. Then, Roethlisberger fumbled after a hit by Charger linebacker Shawne Merriman.

Finally in the second quarter, the offenses gained some momentum. On the sixth play of their opening possession in the quarter, the Steelers thought they had scored the first touchdown of the game when Ward made a diving catch, hopped up, and zigzagged his way to the end zone. The Chargers, though, challenged the play, and the officials ruled that Ward was down by contact at the Chargers' 33. Roethlisberger, undaunted by the reversal, proceeded to hit Randle El for a 21-yard gain, and then Bettis ran for five yards. On the next play, Roethlisberger lined up in the shotgun and ran a masterful quarterback draw, barreling into the end zone from seven yards out.

On the following possession, Chargers quarterback Drew Brees moved the ball to the Steelers' 35. But Pittsburgh linebacker James Harrison ended the drive in a play with movie-reel pizzazz. He snatched a pass that bounced off the hands of Antonio Gates by tipping the ball to himself. He took off in a sprint, hurdling LaDainian Tomlinson on the way, bringing the interception back to the Chargers' 41. Eight plays later—featuring runs of 14 yards by Parker and eight by Roethlisberger—Pittsburgh went ahead 14-0 after Bettis leaped through an open crack on the edge of the end zone. With only 1:37 remaining in the half, the Chargers threw a quick counterpunch. Brees completed passes of 13 yards and 23 yards and then connected with Gates on a **slant pattern** from 11 yards out. The final-seconds touchdown narrowed the Chargers' deficit to 14-7 going into halftime.

In the second half, the Chargers chipped away at the lead. Three field goals by Nate Kaeding put San Diego ahead 16-14 with 11:41 remaining. Roethlisberger responded with three crucial passes—33 and 13 yards to Ward and 16 yards to tight end Heath Miller for the touchdown and a 21-16 lead. The Chargers recaptured the lead with a two-yard touchdown with 4:42 left in the game. When the Chargers failed to make the two-point conversion, San Diego stood on top by one point, 22-21. In the final minutes of the game, Roethlisberger engineered a 33-yard drive to the San Diego 29 when the series suddenly took a costly toll. Roethlisberger's knee buckled after a hit by the Chargers' Luis Castillo. He was helped off the field with 1:05 remaining. With Maddox also sidelined with an injury, No. 3 backup Charlie Batch took over. After three handoffs to Bettis for seven yards, Reed kicked a game-winning field goal with just six seconds left.

Pittsburgh's 24-22 victory at San Diego came with a hefty price. Roethlisberger left the stadium on crutches and was sidelined for Game 5 against the Jacksonville Jaguars with a hyperextended, bruised knee. From his front-row seat, he watched Maddox bloop and blunder. Maddox, who had not started an important game since Week 2 of the previous season, proved to be rusty, fumbling the ball in overtime and throwing three

Ben Roethlisberger's knee buckled during a game in October 2005 after he was hit by the Chargers' defensive end Luis Castillo. Roethlisberger suffered a hyperextended, bruised knee and missed the next game. Knee problems also caused him to miss three games later in the season.

interceptions, the last one returned 41 yards for the game-winning touchdown. The Jaguars came away with a 23-17 win.

For Game 6, Roethlisberger was back, and the Steelers showed the Cincinnati Bengals just how much they had missed him. The offense ran the ball better than it had all season with Willie Parker claiming 131 yards of the Steelers' 221 total rushing yards. Meanwhile, the defense held the Bengals to just three points on their first two possessions, even though they traveled to the Steelers' 12-yard line on their first possession and to the Steelers' 8 on their second. At halftime, Pittsburgh led 7-6 before taking control in the final two quarters. On the Bengals' first two possessions of the second half, quarterback Carson Palmer threw a pair of interceptions. The first was picked off by safety Chris Hope and led to a field goal. The second interception, by defensive end Aaron Smith, resulted in a touchdown to give the Steelers a 17-6 lead. Before this game, Palmer had gone 20 quarters and 169 pass attempts without throwing an interception.

At the end of the third quarter, Pittsburgh scored again, on a four-yard touchdown pass to Hines Ward. Although Roethlisberger did not attempt a pass in the fourth quarter—only throwing for a game-total 93 yards—he used a successful running game to its full potency. On the feet of Parker and Haynes, the Steelers ran the ball 19 times in the fourth quarter, padding their lead with another field goal. With 2:52 remaining, Pittsburgh had a 27-6 lead. After the two-minute warning, Cincinnati tacked on a late-game touchdown, but Pittsburgh rolled away with the win.

On Halloween night, the Steelers squeezed past a close call with the Baltimore Ravens that otherwise could have had a scary ending. Pittsburgh managed a 20-19 win but nearly self-destructed midway through the fourth quarter. On fourth-and-10 from their own 45, Pittsburgh's special teams botched the **snap** on a punt. Wide receiver Sean Morey walked up behind long snapper Greg Warren to warn his teammates that the Ravens had two players on return, including the dangerous Deion Sanders. Not noticing Morey, Warren snapped the ball early, and it smacked into Morey's leg. Quickly, Morey scooped up the loose ball and threw it to punter Chris Gardocki, who passed back to Morey incomplete. The Ravens took over possession at the Steelers' 45 and turned the blunder into a go-ahead field goal, giving Baltimore a 19-17 lead.

With 3:21 left to play, Roethlisberger turned on his football finesse. The final scoring drive included back-to-back completions—14 yards to Randle El and 23 yards to Quincy Morgan. Next, Haynes picked up seven yards on a **draw play**. Bettis took care of the rest with four consecutive carries totaling 16 yards. The drive set up a 37-yard game-winning field goal by Reed.

The win was a relief, but Roethlisberger aggravated his right knee. Pittsburgh was scheduled to play the Green Bay Packers at Lambeau Field the following Sunday, but Roethlisberger's injury made other plans for him.

BACK IN THE HUNT

On November 3, Roethlisberger underwent arthroscopic surgery to repair a torn lateral meniscus (knee cartilage). The Steelers felt some pain of their own in his absence. They started out well with Charlie Batch at the helm, scoring a 20-10 victory over the Packers. In Week 10 (Game 9 for the Steelers), Batch racked up a 17-7 lead over the Browns before sustaining an injury to his throwing hand. On a 15-yard completion to Ward—a play that gave Ward the Steelers' all-time receptions record at 538, Batch's hand smashed into the helmet of a defender, fracturing his pinkie bone. Maddox took over in the second half. Sticking to the running game, he led the offense to 17 more points and a 34-21 victory.

After the game against the Browns, most fans immediately wondered when Roethlisberger would return to action. With Batch out for at least two weeks and Maddox still struggling, everyone was eager to see Roethlisberger back at quarterback. Although he was ahead of schedule in rehabilitation, he was unsure if he would be ready to play in Week 11 against the Ravens. "I don't know yet," he told reporters following Batch's injury, as recorded in *Tough as Steel*. "We got a little urgency now, so we'll see." Unfortunately, Roethlisberger was not fully recovered by game day, and the Steelers were unable to pull off a win.

As the season stood, the Steelers held a 7–3 record—tied for first place in the AFC North Division with the Cincinnati Bengals. The main focus was staying atop the division, but the Steelers seemed to take a downward slide. On November 28 at the RCA Dome in Indianapolis, Roethlisberger returned to the field, but the Steelers became victim No. 11 for the undefeated

Colts. The Colts set the tempo early when quarterback Peyton Manning hit Marvin Harrison for an 80-yard score on the first offensive play. A field goal by Mike Vanderjagt made the score 10-0. The momentum looked as if it might shift when, on the Colts' next possession, Polamalu intercepted Manning's pass and returned it 26 yards to the Indianapolis 7-yard line. After back-to-back false starts, Roethlisberger fired to Hines Ward for a 12-yard touchdown that cut the margin to 10-7 at the end of the first quarter.

From that point on, the Steelers fell apart. A missed 41-yard field goal by Reed, a late second-quarter interception by Roethlisberger, and a game riddled with false-start penalties were only a fraction of the poison. To start the second half, Coach Cowher made a crucial decision to go with an **onside kick**. He hoped it would create a "spark" for his team. The plan went horribly awry, though, leading to another Colts touchdown and making the score 23-7 less than four minutes into the third quarter. "They beat us all the way around," Bettis said in *Tough as Steel*. "They dominated from the word, 'Go.' It was a frustrating night—all the way around." The Steelers' 26-7 loss dropped their record to 7–4, a game behind Cincinnati. If they wanted to make an appearance in the playoffs, their next five games—including battles with the Bengals and the Bears (8–3)—left little margin for error. More than a single loss would likely end their playoff hopes.

Unfortunately, Roethlisberger entered the game against Cincinnati with a severe thumb injury. Although no one would divulge the details of the injury, Roethlisberger admitted that it was "pretty painful." Whether or not the thumb was to blame, he threw a regular-season-high three interceptions, despite posting a hefty 386 passing yards. The Steelers held momentary leads of 7-0 and 14-7 in the first half. Then, trailing in the third quarter, 24-17, a 20-yard touchdown pass to Ward tied the game at 24. The Bengals, though, continued to strike back, going ahead 31-24 late in the third quarter.

Roethlisberger's most costly turnover came in the fourth quarter when the Steelers were trying to drive for what could have been the tying score. His pass, which was intended for Ward, was intercepted and led to an eventual touchdown. On Pittsburgh's next possession, Roethlisberger connected with Ward for a six-yard touchdown, capping off a 10-play, 72-yard drive. With only three minutes remaining, Pittsburgh was unable to muster another touchdown and lost 38-31.

Even though Roethlisberger played with a painful injury, he was not about to use it as an excuse. "We've got a lot of guys dinged up, and we've got to play through pain," he said in an Associated Press article. "Myself included. It hurts, but it was good enough to play." Dropping to 7–5, two games behind the Bengals, the Steelers could not afford another loss.

Luckily, the Steelers' slump was short-lived. On December 11, the Pittsburgh skies delivered the ultimate Steelers' playing conditions at Heinz Field—thick snow and curdling mud. Still wrestling with a bad thumb, Big Ben stuck with risk-free passes. On a day with few errors, Roethlisberger completed 13 of 20 passes for 173 yards and no interceptions in a 21-9 win over the Bears. Bettis—whom Ward described as a "mudder"—ran for 101 yards and two touchdowns. The victory marked a streak-ending day—bringing an end to Pittsburgh's losing streak and the Bears' eight-game winning streak. For the Steelers, victory meant much more, though. Now 8–5, they were in a four-way race for two AFC wild-card berths, trailing the Jaguars (9–4) by a game and tied with the Chiefs (8–5) and the Chargers (8–5).

Next, keeping in stride, the Steelers delivered back-to-back hammerings in Minneapolis and Cleveland. Roethlisberger was in peak performance, throwing 10 of 15 for 149 yards in an 18-3 win over the Vikings. The next week, on December 24, Pittsburgh brought a holiday hammering to the Browns, 41-0. Roethlisberger, going 13 of 20 for 226 yards and a touchdown, sliced up the Browns like Christmas goose. With the victory,

Justin Smith *(bottom)* and Robert Geathers (91) of the Bengals sacked Ben Roethlisberger during the final moments of their game on December 4, 2005. With a 38-31 loss to Cincinnati, the Steelers' record was 7–5, and they were in danger of missing the playoffs.

Pittsburgh upped its record to 10–5, with one pin left to knock down—Detroit.

On January 1, the Steelers made a New Year's resolution to win—they needed a victory to make the playoffs. Although Roethlisberger played a bit under par—completing only 7 of

(continues on page 76)

THE BUS—NO. 36

Jerome "The Bus" Bettis was a key part of the Steelers' offense. In each of his first six seasons with the Steelers, he rushed for more than 1,000 yards. During a span of 10 seasons, Pittsburgh fans fell head over heels for The Bus. On January 1, 2006—the last game of the 2005 regular season, fans realized that this night might be Bettis's last game at Heinz Field. After Pittsburgh pummeled the Detroit Lions 35-21, the crowd begged him to stay with chants of "One More Year!"

Bettis—who grew up in Detroit, Michigan—started his football career at the esteemed University of Notre Dame in 1990. In 1993, he was drafted in the first round, as the tenth pick of the Rams, who were based in Los Angeles at that time. During his rookie year, he rushed for 1,429 yards, becoming the first Rams rookie to rush for more than 1,000 yards since Eric Dickerson in 1983. He also was only one of eight rookies to rush for 200 yards in a single game. His outstanding play earned him the NFL Co-Rookie of the Year, the *Sporting News* Rookie of the Year, a Rams MVP award, and a trip to the Pro Bowl. During his rookie year, he picked up the nickname "Battering Ram," but he soon traded that one in for another.

His days with the Rams ended after a disappointing 1995 season in which he rushed for just 637 yards. In exchange for two second-round draft picks, the Rams traded Bettis to the Pittsburgh Steelers—in what came to be known as the Trade of the Decade. In his first season with the Steelers, Bettis ran for 1,431 yards and 11 touchdowns, including a 220-yard game against his former Ram teammates. He emerged as one of the premier running backs in the NFL. During a Green Bay broadcast, legendary Steelers radio commentator Myron Cope first referred to Bettis as "The Bus." He picked up the name after hearing one of Bettis's Notre Dame buddies call him "Bussy." As one might assume, the nickname had nothing to do with Pittsburgh's black and gold uniform, although it certainly helped the image. The name came from Bettis's ability to carry multiple defenders on his back—like a bus—while rushing.

In a game against the Detroit Lions on Thanksgiving Day 1998, Bettis was caught in the thick of one of the most controversial calls in NFL history. The Steelers sent out Bettis as their representative to call the coin toss to decide who would get the ball first in overtime. Bettis called "tails" when the coin was in the air. Even though the coin landed tails up, the referee insisted that Bettis had called heads and awarded the ball to Detroit. The backward call paved the way for Detroit's victory. After the incident, the NFL altered its coin-toss rules. Now, the call of "heads" or "tails" is made before the coin is tossed, rather than during the toss, and at least two officials must hear the call. Some people jokingly refer to it as the "Jerome Bettis Rule." On an ESPN list of the top-10 worst sports official calls, the coin-toss incident was voted No. 8 by fans.

After 2001, Bettis was unable to reach the magic 1,000-yard mark. However, he still carried his 255-pound weight in gold. In his final two seasons, he rushed for 22 of his 91 career touchdowns. The bus ride ended after winning the 2006 Super Bowl in his hometown of Detroit. Bettis closed his NFL career as a six-time Pro Bowler and as the fifth all-time rusher with 13,662 yards—only one of six players in NFL history to rush for 13,000 yards. He was fourth in rushing attempts with 3,347 and one of eight players to rush for 1,000 yards in eight or more seasons. After Bettis's final game, Super Bowl MVP Hines Ward shouted, "I'm going to Disney World, and I'm taking *The Bus!*"

Ben Roethlisberger and Jerome Bettis celebrated Bettis's third-quarter touchdown in the Steelers' final game of the 2005 season against the Detroit Lions. Bettis rushed for three touchdowns in the 35-21 victory—a win the Steelers needed to make the playoffs.

(continued from page 73)

16 passes for 135 yards and two interceptions—he ran for one touchdown. Bettis picked up the slack with three touchdown runs in what was probably his last game at Heinz Field. Special teams also added to the 35-21 win. Randle El pocketed an 81-yard touchdown on a punt return, and cornerback Ricardo Colclough returned a kickoff 63 yards to set up another touchdown. Despite a rough and tumble year—laden with errors and injuries, the Steelers muscled their way back for another

day, winning their last four games of the regular season. Next stop—the playoffs.

In a second run at the playoffs, 23-year-old Roethlisberger felt he was better prepared this time. "Last year, I was kind of, 'Oh my gosh, I'm so nervous. Don't make a mistake,' " he said in *Tough as Steel*. "I'm not going to go out and play not to make a mistake this year. I'm going to go out to win football games and play as good as I can to help this team win."

Lucky No. 40

The Steelers had made it into the postseason the hard way—playing catch-up. The toughest road, however, was still before them. In each conference, six teams make the playoffs. The Steelers were the No. 6, or lowest, seed in the **American Football Conference**. Only one team in NFL history had made it to the Super Bowl winning all three playoff games on the road—the 1985 New England Patriots. In the 2005 season, Pittsburgh faced the same challenge.

On January 8, 2006, the Steelers met their first opponent—their division rival, the Bengals—at Paul Brown Stadium in Cincinnati, Ohio. The Bengals pounced to a 10-0 lead early in the game. On the first drive, quarterback Carson Palmer connected with rookie wideout Chris Henry on a 66-yard pass. The crowd's enthusiasm quickly waned, though, when they realized that Palmer had been hurt on the play. Pittsburgh's Kimo von Oelhoffen, who had taken Palmer down, got his arm tangled around Palmer's leg and bent it awkwardly while crawling forward. The injury turned out to be a serious one—a torn anterior cruciate ligament (ACL)—a knee injury that took the Pro Bowl quarterback out of the game. Backup quarterback Jon Kitna drove the Bengals to the Steelers' 5-yard line, after a completion to T.J. Houshmandzadeh, but the Bengals failed to get a touchdown. They settled for a field goal and a 3-0 lead in a costly drive that banged up the offense—Henry also injured his knee during the possession.

On the next possession, the Steelers were forced to punt. The Bengals—now led by Kitna—drove 76 yards in seven plays, the final play being a 20-yard touchdown run by Rudi Johnson. On the following drive, the Steelers struck back with a touchdown. On the scoring play, Roethlisberger led a perfectly executed screen pass to Willie Parker. Parker let Bengal linebacker Brian Simmons get by him and slipped to his right. Roethlisberger delivered the pass on the **flat**. Cincinnati struck back with a seven-yard touchdown pass to Houshmandzadeh. An unsportsmanlike conduct call on Troy Polamalu helped set up the touchdown by turning a fourth and 11 at the Steelers' 17-yard line into first and goal at the 8. The call came after Polamalu threw a punch at Bengals center Rich Braham. Turning up the heat, the Steelers made it 17-14 before the half when Roethlisberger nailed Cedrick Wilson on a 54-yard pass and then found Hines Ward for a five-yard touchdown pass.

Holding an early lead, the Bengals should have harnessed the momentum. They spent too much time, however, dwelling on Palmer's injury. In the second half, the game unraveled for the Bengals. Kicker Shayne Graham botched a field goal that would have increased the Bengals' lead to 20-14. Instead, the Steelers took over at their own 34-yard line. Capping off the ensuing drive, Jerome Bettis sidestepped Bengals corner Troy

Ben Roethlisberger ran off the field after the Steelers' 31-17 win over the Bengals on January 8, 2006, in the first round of the playoffs. Roethlisberger had a stellar game, completing 14 of 19 passes for 208 yards, with three touchdowns and no interceptions.

James for a touchdown run. The Steelers took a 21-17 lead that they never relinquished. On defense, Pittsburgh laid siege on Kitna, forcing two interceptions. A Roethlisberger-led offense scored two more times with a field goal and a touchdown. The touchdown drive concluded with a trick play, in which Randle El took the direct snap and passed it back to Roethlisberger.

Roethlisberger hit a wide-open Cedrick Wilson for a 43-yard score. In a phenomenal 31-17 win, Roethlisberger completed 14 of 19 passes for 208 yards, three touchdowns, no interceptions, and a nearly perfect 148.7 passer rating. The Steelers proved that, although they might have had to claw their way to the playoffs, they certainly belonged there.

Around the NFL, however, many still had doubts. The Steelers entered the AFC Divisional Game as 9½-point underdogs to the top-seeded Colts. Big Ben played a brilliant, unexpected passing game, using both his arm and head. Even though the Steelers' offensive strength lay in its varied running game, Roethlisberger's wide-open passing stole the show. On Pittsburgh's first possession, Roethlisberger led an 84-yard, 10-play scoring drive that featured seven passes, including a 36-yarder and an 18-yarder to tight end Heath Miller. Later in the first quarter, Hines Ward broke two tackles on a 45-yard completion. A seven-yard touchdown pass to Miller gave the Steelers a 14-0 lead at the end of the first. "The play-calling was aggressive," Ward said after the game, as quoted by the Associated Press. "They (the football community) thought all we can do is run the ball. We can pass the ball, too." In the second quarter, the Colts marched 96 yards in 15 plays, in a drive that ate up nearly 10 minutes. But what would be Peyton Manning's best drive of the game—going 6-for-6—ended with a hollow 20-yard field goal.

Pittsburgh continued to dominate in the second half. Manning faced a rush of linebackers, ends, and blitzing backs from the Steelers' ferocious defense. He was nearly sacked for a safety in the third quarter, when he was downed at the 1-yard line. The Colts had to punt after the sack, and the Steelers' possession led to Bettis's one-yard touchdown run—his eleventh touchdown of the season—making the score 21-3 at the end of the third period. Going into the fourth quarter, it looked as though the Steelers had the game all wrapped up. The only thing missing was the bow. Then, early in the fourth quarter, Manning connected on a 50-yard pass to Dallas Clark, cutting Pittsburgh's lead to 21-10. And the final five minutes were filled with gut-wrenching twists and one tide-turning play after another.

With 5:26 remaining, Polamalu made a diving interception off of Manning at the Pittsburgh 48-yard line. As he got up to run, he fumbled the ball and recovered it again. In a controversial call by referee Pete Morelli, the possession was overturned. According to Morelli, Polamalu never had possession of the ball, even though replays clearly showed otherwise. Manning took advantage of his second chance by connecting on a 20-yarder to Marvin Harrison and a 24-yarder to Reggie Wayne. Colts running back Edgerrin James ran in for the touchdown. Manning then completed a two-point conversion pass to Wayne, bringing the score to a close 21-18.

On its next possession, Pittsburgh was forced to punt. But with 1:20 left in the game, Manning was sacked for the fifth time on **fourth down** at the Colts' 2-yard line. On most days, the game would have been over. This day, however, had proven that anything could happen. The sure-handed Bettis popped an uncharacteristic goal-line fumble. Indianapolis's Nick Harper grabbed the football and took off downfield for a possible game-winning touchdown. The save came from Big Ben. A diving Roethlisberger reached out and yanked down Harper at the Indy 42-yard line. "Once in a blue moon, Jerome fumbles," Roethlisberger later told the Associated Press, "Once in a blue moon, I make a tackle. They just happened to be in the same game." Two Manning passes later, with the ball at the Pittsburgh 27, kicker Mike Vanderjagt lined up for a 46-yard field goal to send the game into overtime. The kick sailed wide right, sealing a victory for the Steelers.

Roethlisberger, who was 14 of 24 for 197 yards, with two touchdowns and one interception, became the first quarterback of the Super Bowl era to reach a Conference Championship Game in his first two seasons in the league.

With just about a minute left in the Steelers' divisional playoff game against the Indianapolis Colts, Ben Roethlisberger made a key tackle to prevent Nick Harper from scoring a touchdown. Harper had recovered a goal-line fumble by Jerome Bettis.

The Steelers also became the first No. 6 seed in NFL history to make it to a conference final. The Steelers were proving that they had just as much game as a top-seeded team. "Ya'll want to come in now?" Roethlisberger said after the win in *Tough as Steel*, directed toward all the people who never expected Pittsburgh to make it this far. "All the non-believers. You want to come in now?"

The upset against the Colts at the RCA Dome in Indianapolis was merely practice for the AFC Championship Game. On January 22, the Steelers bucked the second-seeded Broncos (who were on a nine-game winning streak at home) at Mile High Stadium in Denver. Pittsburgh jumped to a 24-3 half-time lead, scoring on all four of its first-half possessions. Jeff Reed started the scoring with a 47-yard field goal, following a 12-play, 62-yard drive. At the start of the second quarter, Roethlisberger hit Wilson in the corner of the end zone with a 12-yard touchdown pass. Next possession, Bettis muscled in from three yards out. The Steelers added another seven points following a painful interception thrown by Broncos quarter-back Jake Plummer. As the first half was coming to a close, Roethlisberger sidestepped the pass rush and bulleted the ball deep in the end zone to Ward.

Instead of pulling out a comeback, Denver just kept making mistakes—four turnovers to Pittsburgh's none. Plummer coughed up his final fumble with 4:52 remaining and the Broncos trailing 27-17. The Steelers took over at the Broncos' 17, and the rest was history. Five plays later, Roethlisberger ran a **bootleg** left for a four-yard touchdown that plumped up Pittsburgh's lead to 34-17 and ended the Broncos home-winning streak.

Riding on the arm of Roethlisberger, the Steelers made history, becoming the first No. 6-seeded team in NFL history to win three consecutive road playoff games. They were also the first team to beat the No. 1, No. 2, and No. 3 seeds in the playoffs. Against Denver, Big Ben completed 21 of 29 for 275 yards and two touchdowns, finishing with a 124.9 passer rating. He converted eight of the first ten third-down conversions. In *Tough as Steel*, right guard Kendall Simmons said, "Ben's playing Elway-like," referring to the only quarterback in Broncos history to lead Denver to a Super Bowl title. "He's a second-year guy, but it's like he's been around forever. He just set the tone for everything."

Finally, after losing in their previous three AFC finals (in 1997, 2001, and 2004), the Pittsburgh Steelers had earned a trip to the Super Bowl. "We've been knocking on this door for years," cornerback Deshea Townsend said in *Tough as Steel*. "We decided that it was time to quit knocking. We came here and just kicked it in."

Roethlisberger was one game away from fulfilling his promise to Bettis. Almost as if fate had planned it, Super Bowl XL was being held in Detroit—Bettis's hometown. In a season fueled by physical endurance, tough comebacks, unbelievable upsets, and in some cases, crazy luck, the Steelers must have wondered if they could make No. 40 their lucky number. Perhaps instead they had their money on No. 7. "Composed, in control, our leader," Bettis said about Roethlisberger. "He's our guy."

MISSION ACCOMPLISHED

At the outset, the Super Bowl energy seemed to favor Seattle, the **National Football Conference** champion. The Seahawks dominated the time of possession in the first quarter, yet endured a tough break. Near the end of the quarter, Seattle quarterback Matt Hasselbeck hit Darrell Jackson for what appeared to be a 17-yard touchdown. Instead, though, a pass-interference penalty was called on Jackson, who (very slightly) pushed off of free safety Chris Hope in the end zone. This illegal move brought the ball back, and Seattle was unable to return to the end zone. The Seahawks settled for a field goal and went into the second quarter with a 3-0 lead—their one short moment of glory.

Until this point, the Steelers had not put up much of a fight. In the first quarter, Seattle's Jackson had caught five passes for 50 yards—33 more yards than the entire Steelers offense. Roethlisberger's numbers hardly resembled those of a Super Bowl quarterback—1 of 5 for one sliver of a yard. Something had to change, and luckily it did.

The momentum shifted in the second quarter, and toward the end of the period, Roethlisberger dove into the end zone for Pittsburgh's first score. To start the second half, the Steelers took over the ball at their own 25-yard line. On the second play, Willie Parker took a handoff from Roethlisberger. Following the path made by a crushing block from offensive lineman Alan Faneca, Parker just escaped a diving tackle attempt by Seattle's Michael Boulware. From that point on, he was untouchable, running 75 yards for a touchdown—the longest touchdown run in Super Bowl history.

Then, toward the middle of the third quarter, the game almost took a nasty turn. With the score at 14-3 and Pittsburgh staring down the chance to secure a Super Bowl victory, Roethlisberger made a crucial mistake. On third and goal at the Seattle 7, he underthrew Cedrick Wilson, and defensive back Kelly Herndon was there to snatch the ball up. Herndon took off downfield, returning the ball 76 yards before Ward made a heroic tackle at the Pittsburgh 20. Herndon's run was the longest interception return in 40 years of the Super Bowl. The Steelers had been driving to the goal and could have gone up 17-3, or 21-3. Instead, it became a four-point game three plays later when tight end Jerramy Stevens reeled in a 16-yard touchdown catch.

With 10:54 remaining in the game, Seattle still had a chance to take the lead, trailing only 14-10. And the Seahawks were again closing in on the end zone. Next, though, it was Hasselbeck's turn to make a mistake. On third and 18, on the Pittsburgh 27-yard line, Hasselbeck floated a pass over the head of Jackson. Cornerback Ike Taylor plucked it out of the air. A few minutes later, the Steelers pulled off their best gimmick play—when Antwaan Randle El passed to Hines Ward—for

Ben Roethlisberger and Jerome Bettis share an emotional moment after the Steelers' Super Bowl XL win in Bettis's hometown of Detroit, Michigan. The previous year, after Pittsburgh lost in the AFC Championship Game, Roethlisberger told Bettis to come back for one more season, promising him a trip to the Super Bowl.

a third touchdown and a guaranteed 21-10 victory. Offensive coordinator Ken Whisenhunt liked to try trick plays, such as the one executed at the Super Bowl. Like Randle El, Hines Ward also played quarterback in college. Their history gave Whisenhunt enormous flexibility. On this night, Whisenhunt saw the Steelers facing the right defense, and it looked like the right time to try one of those plays. In the most important game of the year, the Steelers pulled off the reverse pass they had rigorously practiced for most of the year. All that practice suddenly seemed well worth it.

Seattle could do nothing on its next possession and had to punt. Pittsburgh settled in to run off some time. With less than four minutes to go, on third and three, Big Ben ran and picked up a huge first down. The Steelers worked the clock—running down another two minutes—all but sealing the victory. As the final seconds ticked away, Bill Cowher laughed and threw his arms around his players on the sideline. After 10 trips to the playoffs in his 14 seasons as coach, he finally led his hometown team to a Super Bowl title. To make the win even more momentous, it was the fifth Super Bowl victory—the "one for the thumb"—for the Steelers. As Cowher's players dumped a cooler of Gatorade over his shoulders, he thrust his fists into the air. Then, he cried—along with most of the Steelers.

Perhaps for Roethlisberger, the enormity of the win did not sink in all at once. His first thoughts were for the rest of the team, especially Jerome "The Bus" Bettis—who finally realized his ultimate dream after 13 seasons in the NFL. Roethlisberger's

ONE FOR THE THUMB

In the days leading up to Super Bowl XL, a lot of Pittsburgh fans were chanting, "One for the thumb!" The idea behind this phrase is really quite simple. If a team were to win five Super Bowls, counting the victories on your fingers would take up an entire hand, with the last win being the thumb.

That fifth Super Bowl title had been elusive for the Steelers. They had waited not-so-patiently since 1980, the days of Terry Bradshaw, Franco Harris, and Jack Lambert. With their "One for the Thumb," the Steelers joined the ranks of the San Francisco 49ers and the Dallas Cowboys as the only teams to win five Super Bowls.

hefty promise fulfilled, he said after the game, "It was absolutely awesome to come up here and win one for Jerome." Likewise, Bettis could breathe a sigh of relief. "I came back to win a championship," he said in *Tough as Steel*. "Mission accomplished. With that, I have to bid farewell." Immediately after the Super Bowl, Bettis retired from the NFL. Returning to his hometown—the Motor City—and becoming a world champion was the exclamation point on his career. He decided that "the Bus's last stop is here in Detroit."

While Bettis closed the cover on his career with a storybook ending, Big Ben was living out a storybook beginning. In his second season in the NFL, he brought his team to the Super Bowl and earned a victory. And he was just getting started.

After the Super Bowl, Roethlisberger was elevated to superstar status. He had to learn how to deal with a whole new world. Until then, all he generally had to think about was the game. Now, he had the added pressure of living under a magnifying glass. His actions would reflect on the entire Pittsburgh team, so he had to be careful how he portrayed himself in the public eye.

Looking for a Replay

It is no big secret. Quarterbacks can get injured in the NFL, sometimes seriously. Already as a young quarterback, Ben Roethlisberger had seen his share of injuries, but this time was different. This one was off the field.

On the late morning of June 12, 2006, Roethlisberger was cruising down Second Avenue in Pittsburgh on his new 2005 Suzuki Hayabusa—a cycle known for speed and power. He was nearing Tenth Street when a woman driving a Chrysler New Yorker pulled into the intersection. Roethlisberger's cycle slammed into the passenger door. He flew off the bike, hit the windshield hard, and then bounced onto the pavement. For a moment, he lay motionless. One witness thought he was dead. Blood pooled on the road, draining out of a nine-inch gash on the back of his head. Then, he regained consciousness.

An ambulance rushed him to Mercy Hospital in Pittsburgh. In addition to the laceration on his head, he had a broken jaw, a crushed sinus cavity, and a handful of missing teeth. He also had some minor knee injuries from hitting the pavement. Luckily, however, the broken jaw was the most serious of his injuries. His brain, spine, chest, and abdomen had been spared. At the time, Roethlisberger did not grasp just how lucky he was to be alive, especially because he was not wearing a helmet. While recovering from seven hours of surgery to repair the fractures in his face, he would have some time to think about it, though.

Back in the summer of 2005, tight end Kellen Winslow of the Cleveland Browns tore some knee ligaments in a motorcycle accident. He too was helmet-free, and his injuries kept him sidelined for the entire 2005 season. At that time, the accident had brought Roethlisberger's habits under the microscope. Roethlisberger openly admitted that he did not wear a helmet when riding, claiming in an interview with ESPN's Andrea Kremer, "You're just more free when you're out there with no helmet on." In Pennsylvania, it is not against the law to ride without one, so Roethlisberger legally had a choice. Unlike Winslow's contract, Roethlisberger's contract does not explicitly prohibit him from riding a cycle, although all NFL players' contracts *do* contain standard clauses about avoiding dangerous activities.

After Winslow's accident, coach Bill Cowher had cautioned Roethlisberger about riding a motorcycle, especially without a helmet. "We talked about being a risk-taker, and I'm not really a risk-taker," Roethlisberger said, "I'm pretty conservative and laid-back, but the big thing is just to be careful. I'll just continue to be careful." At that point, Roethlisberger only rode Harleys and Choppers—the Cadillacs of motorcycles. He rode for relaxation, not adventure. He was confident in his ability to ride a motorcycle, and he truly believed such an accident would not

A Pittsburgh police officer assisted in the investigation of an accident on June 12, 2006, between a car and a motorcycle driven by Ben Roethlisberger. The Steelers' quarterback, who was not wearing a helmet, suffered a broken jaw and a crushed sinus cavity in the collision. He was in surgery for seven hours to repair the fractures to his face.

happen to him. At training camp in 2005, former Steeler Terry Bradshaw, who quarterbacked the team to their four other Super Bowl victories in the 1970s, gave Roethlisberger some fatherly advice: "Ride it when you retire."

After hearing news of the accident, players and fans gathered at Mercy Hospital. Cowher arrived around 9:20 that night. Of course, their first concerns were for Roethlisberger's condition. They were there to be supportive. However, they also wanted some news about his recovery time. Would he be ready to play at the start of the NFL season in September? According to the doctors, his broken jaw would heal in about seven weeks—in plenty of time for the season opener.

Shortly after he was released from the hospital on June 15, Roethlisberger made a public apology. "In the past few days, I have gained a new perspective on life," he said in an article by the Associated Press. "By the grace of God, I am fortunate to be alive. . . . I am sorry for any anxiety and concern my actions have caused others, specifically my family, the Steelers organization, my teammates, and our fans." The incident was a turning point for Roethlisberger and sparked a change in his behavior. "I recognize that I have a responsibility to safeguard my health in the off-season so I can continue to lead our team effectively," he said and added a promise. "If I ever ride again, it certainly will be with a helmet." And as Jerome Bettis would attest, Roethlisberger knew how to keep a promise.

ROCKY SEASON

As doctors predicted, Roethlisberger made a quick recovery from the accident. However, an emergency appendectomy on Sunday, September 3, kept him from playing the season opener at Heinz Field. Sadly, Roethlisberger missed a pretty grand ceremony—the unveiling of the five Super Bowl championship banners, complete with pregame fireworks and an in-stadium concert. Still, backup Charlie Batch did a good job of managing the team in his absence, leading the Steelers to a 28-17 win over Miami.

The game pivoted on one crucial play by tight end Heath Miller. Midway through the fourth quarter, Miller charged down the sideline for an 87-yard touchdown pass. The replay, however, showed that the touchdown was actually no good. Miller had stepped out of bounds between the 1- and 2-yard lines. But Dolphin coach Nick Saban hesitated in throwing his red **coach's challenge** flag. It was a costly delay, with the flag falling to the turf unseen by officials until it was too late. By the time they saw it, the extra point had been kicked. According to the rules, once the next play has started, a coach can no longer challenge a call. The gift touchdown took a close four-point

SWISS MISTER

The trip to Detroit for Super Bowl XL may have been the trip of a lifetime for Ben Roethlisberger and the Steelers. A few months after that game, Roethlisberger took another trip—a trip, perhaps, of several lifetimes. In May 2006, he, his parents, and his sister traveled to Switzerland to visit the home of their ancestors who immigrated to the United States. Besides stops in the bigger cities of Bern, Lucerne, and Zurich, the Roethlisbergers visited the farming community of Lauperswil in the Emmental region of Switzerland. Ben Roethlisberger's great-great-grandfather, Karl Roethlisberger, left Lauperswil in 1873 to come to the United States to seek a better life.

"I only recently began researching my personal Swiss roots, but I'm making up for lost time," Ben said before the trip. The document that permitted Karl Roethlisberger to come to the United States showed that he was 32, blue-eyed and balding, and had no outstanding debts. In Lauperswil, Ben's father, Ken, said, "When we came over the hill, we realized he probably looked at these very same things. I can see how a person could live here. It's amazing."

Roethlisberger's trip was part of a special Swiss Roots campaign organized by the Swiss government and its tourism board. The aim of the campaign is to reach out to the more than one million Americans who have Swiss ancestry.

game and turned it into a guaranteed victory for the Steelers. Still, it was a 1–0 start for Pittsburgh in 2006.

In Week 2, Big Ben was back in the Steelers' lineup but not in prime form. Barely two weeks after his appendectomy, Roethlisberger had his midsection wrapped in protective padding. However, it did not save him from the pain. The Jacksonville Jaguars made him pay for his courage. Over the course of the game, he was sacked twice and knocked down several other times. On his final hit, Roethlisberger wobbled to the sideline, clutching his side and wincing. In a 9-0 shutout, Pittsburgh tallied only 26 rushing yards, and Roethlisberger hit 17 of 32 passes, with two interceptions. It was the lowest scoring game in the history of *Monday Night Football*. Perhaps Cowher should have kept Roethlisberger out of harm's way. On Sunday, Roethlisberger had woken up feeling sick and had registered a fever earlier on Monday. But Cowher wanted him to play and to get him ready, as well, for next week's game against division rival Cincinnati.

There was little Cowher could do to prepare the Steelers for the wrath of Carson Palmer, though. After Kimo von Oelhoffen tore apart his knee in the playoffs the previous season, Palmer endured eight grueling months of rehabilitation. He marched onto Heinz Field on September 24 to prove that paybacks can be tough. The Steelers' game was littered with turnovers, special-teams errors, and mental mistakes, including an early interception in the end zone and a botched punt return late in the game. With four touchdown passes and a 28-20 victory over Pittsburgh, Palmer got his revenge. The Steelers dropped to 1–2.

After a bye week, the Steelers traveled across the country to Qualcomm Stadium in San Diego, California. Roethlisberger waged battle against his 2004 draft rival Philip Rivers. With two touchdown passes—one to polish off a 91-yard drive, Rivers was up to the challenge. He handed Roethlisberger his third straight loss. "I can't tell you the last time I lost three games in a row," said Roethlisberger, who threw two interceptions in the game and was sacked five times. "I feel like I have let my teammates down and let the fans down," he said after the game. "I know I can play better, and I know I will." Roethlisberger knew he would have to get on track if he wanted to make another Super Bowl appearance.

On October 15, back home at Heinz Field, Roethlisberger kept yet another promise. He threw his first two touchdown passes since the AFC Championship Game in a 45-7 pummeling of the Kansas City Chiefs. The fans all agreed that he had definitely played better, racking up 31 points in the first half. Going into the game, Roethlisberger sat among the lowest-rated NFL quarterbacks, with no touchdown passes and seven interceptions. His strategy against the Chiefs was simple. "I tried throwing to the guys in the black shirts rather than the guys in the white shirts," he joked in a post-game interview. Roethlisberger played sharp and polished, completing 16 of 19 passes for 238 yards.

The following week, the Steelers appeared to be on their way to another blowout, this time against the Atlanta Falcons. Before the half, Roethlisberger was already 15 of 20 for 235 yards and three touchdowns. He appeared unstoppable. Then, early in the third quarter, he took a scary helmet-to-helmet blow from Chauncey Davis after releasing a pass. The hit knocked him unconscious. He remained laid out on the turf for at least five minutes before hobbling to the sideline. Moments later, he rode the cart back to the locker room. Suffering a concussion, Roethlisberger later emerged dressed in street clothes. For the rest of the game, Atlanta took advantage of every Pittsburgh mistake, hanging on to take the game into overtime. From the sideline, there was little Roethlisberger could do to help his teammates. He simply had to watch as Falcon kicker Morten Andersen cleared the game-winning field goal, handing Pittsburgh a painful 41-38 loss.

The season went from bad to worse over the next couple of weeks. Four turnovers, four personal fouls, and five sacks led to a 20-13 loss to Oakland. Roethlisberger, still recovering from his concussion, threw interceptions on two of Pittsburgh's first three possessions. And it was déjà vu in the fourth quarter as he tossed two more interceptions when the Steelers were driving for a potential tying score. Embarrassed and frustrated, Roethlisberger commented, "In my wildest dreams, I didn't think I'd be playing this bad." The mistakes continued, and a six-turnover, 31-20 loss to Denver in Week 9 ended any realistic chance for the Steelers to repeat as Super Bowl champions. Their 2–6 record matched the worst midseason record in Bill Cowher's 15-season career. It was also the worst by any returning NFL champion in 20 years. No team in NFL history had ever come back from a 2–6 record and a loss in its eighth game to make the playoffs. Only the Arizona Cardinals, at 1–7, had a worse record. The Steelers would have to sweep their final eight games to pull out a 10–6 record. Perhaps that would be the magic number to reach the AFC playoffs. However, something would have to change. The Steelers had more turnovers in their last two games (10) than they did in their eight-game winning streak that ended the previous season and carried through the playoffs. With 24 turnovers, they also had more in a half-season than in all of last season (23).

The big question circling Heinz Field on November 12 was, "Could they do it?" Thanks to a pregame meeting, Pittsburgh's future appeared hopeful. Instead of Coach Cowher controlling the floor, he opened it up to team leaders. Players expressed their frustrations in a session that left some of them in tears. After giving away a big lead, the Steelers rallied to a 38-31 win over the New Orleans Saints. Roethlisberger threw three touchdown passes and no interceptions, and Willie Parker rushed for 213 yards, including runs of 72 and 76 yards in the second half that set up two touchdowns. Still, it was only one victory. They had to keep the momentum rolling. And it

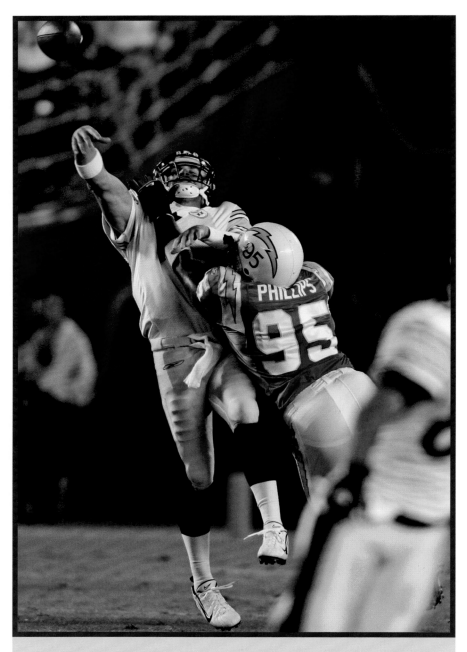

Chargers linebacker Shaun Phillips hit Ben Roethlisberger as he released a pass during the fourth quarter of a game on October 8, 2006. The pass was intercepted. As the Steelers got off to a 2–6 start, Roethlisberger was plagued by interceptions.

rolled into Cleveland Browns Stadium at just the right time the following week. After throwing three interceptions in the first half, Roethlisberger struck when his team needed him the most. He threw for 272 yards, 224 of which were in the fourth quarter. Tacking on 21 points in the final period, the Steelers avoided a deadly defeat. Just minutes away from being kicked into the basement of the AFC North, Roethlisberger improvised a brilliant play. Scrambling, he tossed a four-yard shovel pass to Willie Parker for the game-winning touchdown with 32 seconds left.

Week 12 took the Steelers to Baltimore, where they could not pull out a fourth-quarter comeback. In fact, they could not even score a touchdown in a brutal 27-0 loss to the Ravens. Roethlisberger was sacked nine times, including a vicious hit by Bart Scott in the second quarter that took Big Ben out of the game for one play. The Ravens' rushing defense harassed him all afternoon. In four of the Steelers' first six drives, they went three and out. The seventh drive concluded with a sack and a fumble that was returned 57 yards for a touchdown.

Nearly out of the running, the Steelers held on to a slender shred of hope that they might still snatch a wild-card berth. They won their next three games, bringing their record to a level 7–7. These games did include a few crowning moments. In a 27-7 victory over the Cleveland Browns, Parker set a Steelers single-game rushing record with 223 yards. During a 97-yard drive, Parker ran 26 yards on five carries. Roethlisberger wrapped up that drive with a 49-yard touchdown pass to Nate Washington. Later, Big Ben capped off a 91-yard drive with a two-yard bootleg touchdown run. He confused the Browns defense, who expected the ball to go to Parker.

In Week 16, however, the Baltimore Ravens inflicted the fatal blow on the Steelers' season. In a 31-7 blowout, the Ravens sent Pittsburgh packing and took over the throne as the new NFL title favorite with a 12–3 record. At least the Steelers ended 2006 on a high note with a 23-17 win in Cincinnati. The victory knocked the Bengals out as playoff contenders and gave the Steelers an 8–8 finish to a rocky season. The Steelers delivered a win for Bill Cowher in his last game as an NFL coach. At the end of the 2006 season, he announced that he was stepping down after 15 years as coach. Under Cowher, the Steelers had compiled a record of 161–99–1, including playoff games. The team won eight division titles, earned 10 playoff berths, advanced to the conference championship game six times, and made two Super Bowl appearances—winning one. Pittsburgh would miss him.

A New Era

It took the Pittsburgh Steelers a few weeks after Bill Cowher resigned as their coach to find his replacement. On January 22, 2007, the Steelers announced that they had hired Mike Tomlin, who had been the defensive coordinator for the Minnesota Vikings in 2006, as their next coach. Like Cowher when he was hired in 1992, Tomlin was also 34 and had also been a defensive coordinator. "The one thing that set him apart was his character, his personality," team president Art Rooney II said. "The more we talked with him the more comfortable we got."

Ben Roethlisberger appeared to be pretty comfortable, too, with his new coach early on. During a mini-camp in May 2007, Roethlisberger said, "Coach Tomlin likes to have fun with the guys. I think the guys are more receptive to that.

Mike Tomlin, the new coach of the Pittsburgh Steelers, and Ben Roethlisberger shared a laugh during a team workout on July 29, 2007, at St. Vincent College in Latrobe, Pennsylvania. Tomlin and Roethlisberger seemed to establish a good rapport from the beginning.

They feel more comfortable being able to communicate with that type of coaching."

In their first games without Cowher, the Steelers blitzed and bulldozed their way to a 3-0 start, which was better than the previous season. Game 4, though dished out a dose of déjà vu.

At the University of Phoenix Stadium in Arizona, the Cardinals shut down the Steelers' high-scoring offense and handed them their first loss.

By October 7, the Steelers had made a full recovery from their encounter with the Cardinals. They took their frustration out on Seattle, pummeling the Seahawks 21-0. The offense took nearly the entire first half to warm up, but once it did, it was unstoppable. With improvising creativity, Roethlisberger led three successive, clock-munching touchdown drives and completed 13 consecutive passes. In the second half, the Steelers had possession of the ball for 24:53, Seattle only 5:07. It was one of the few times a shutout could be credited to the offense as much as the defense. In the Steelers' first five games, the defense allowed only a total of 47 points, the fourth fewest points allowed in franchise history—just behind 1937 (38), 1936 (40), and 1934 (45).

The Steelers were 4–1 going into the bye week. But the extra practice time couldn't buy them a win on October 21 at Mile High Stadium in Denver. The Broncos forced three turnovers—one that was returned for a touchdown—and sacked Big Ben four times. Until this game, Pittsburgh had allowed just five touchdowns all season. In Week 7, the Steelers surrendered four touchdowns in one game. By end of the third quarter, Pittsburgh was down 28-14. Then, Roethlisberger directed a 94-yard drive, ending with a 13-yard touchdown grab by Matt Spaeth. Later, he led a 78-yard drive, completing all eight passes and hitting Heath Miller for a 12-yard touchdown strike, to tie the game with 1:10 remaining. Pittsburgh could not hang on, though. Bronco kicker Jason Elam cleared a game-winning 49-yard field goal as time expired, sending Pittsburgh to a deflating 31-28 loss.

On October 28 at Paul Brown Stadium, a conservative call by Cincinnati's coach, Marvin Lewis, worked in Pittsburgh's favor. Trailing 14-3, the Bengals drove to fourth and one, just inside the 2-yard line, with 2:16 left in the second quarter. They needed only two more feet to nab the first down. The largest crowd in stadium history all wanted the Bengals to go for it; so did the players. Instead of having faith in his offense, though, Lewis decided to play it safe and kick a field goal instead of flexing some muscle and going for the touchdown. Instead of a possible score of 14-10, Cincinnati settled for 14-6. Lewis's decision had a ripple effect that ultimately ended in a 24-13 loss to the Steelers. On the ensuing drive, Pittsburgh showed the Bengals how it was done. Roethlisberger drove to Cincinnati's

BIG BEN LOVES ANIMALS

Ben Roethlisberger feels that he has been blessed in his life with opportunities to pursue his goals and achieve success in those pursuits. In 2006, he established the Ben Roethlisberger Foundation in an effort to help those who might be less fortunate. The mission of the foundation is to provide support for police and fire departments throughout the United States. He chose to focus on service dogs. "My dad instilled in me a love and respect for animals," Roethlisberger said on his Web site. "This is a good way to combine that passion with a desire to support the police and fire departments."

Roethlisberger especially donates to departments in his two hometowns—Findlay, Ohio, and Pittsburgh, Pennsylvania. In 2006, the newly formed foundation gave its first grant to help the Findlay Police Department. The officers there had recently lost their service dog, Skip, when he was tragically shot to death. Part of Roethlisberger's grant went to purchase a K-9 ballistic vest. Many police departments do not have enough money in their budgets to purchase protective vests for their service dogs.

1-yard line with nine seconds to go in the half. He confidently handed off to Willie Parker, who dove into the end zone to beef up the Steelers' lead to 21-6. Roethlisberger finished 19 of 26 for 230 yards and only one costly mistake, a forced interception midway through the third quarter. The Bengals responded with a 17-play drive that ended with a nine-yard touchdown, lessening their deficit to 21-13. On their next possession, Pittsburgh tacked on a field goal, and Cincinnati never answered back.

In 2007, grants were distributed to support or purchase service dogs (and vests) to assist police officers and firefighters. The grants went to departments in and around Pittsburgh, as well as in the cities and surrounding communities of each regular-season away game. These cities were Cleveland, Phoenix, Denver, Cincinnati, New York/New Jersey, Boston, St. Louis, and Baltimore. Also in 2007, the Marathon Oil Company donated $1,000 to the Ben Roethlisberger Foundation for every touchdown run or pass Big Ben made in the season. As of Week 16, Roethlisberger had 34 of these touchdowns, bringing in a hefty $34,000 donation.

In addition to the Ben Roethlisberger Foundation, Big Ben donates to other charitable causes. He is especially involved in promoting youth sports in various school districts. Following the devastating Indian Ocean tsunami of December 26, 2004, he announced that he would donate his $18,000 playoff check to the relief effort and challenged other players to do the same. Part of what makes Roethlisberger a great NFL player is that he sincerely wants to make a difference off the field as well as on.

THUNDERING RALLY

There was a little magic in the air at Heinz Field on the night of November 5. As part of the Steelers' 75th-season celebration, past greats like Jack Ham, Franco Harris, and Terry Bradshaw had special seats at the game. In the past, Baltimore had beaten up on Pittsburgh. It's hard to bully fate, though, and this time, fate was waving a Terrible Towel. Pittsburgh owned the first half. Roethlisberger tied the Steelers' single-game record with five touchdown passes, all before halftime. The Steel Curtain defense forced four turnovers in the first half, as well. On Baltimore's first possession, James Harrison leveled quarterback Steve McNair, forcing a fumble that Pittsburgh recovered at the 20. After the snap, Roethlisberger stepped out of the Raven pass rush to hit Miller with a 17-yard touchdown pass. Later, on a first quarter punt return, Harrison hit All-Pro safety Ed Reed so hard the ball flew nearly 15 feet before the Steelers recovered it. Four plays later, Roethlisberger found Santonio Holmes for a 15-yard touchdown pass. Pittsburgh held a dominating 28-point lead at the half. In the third quarter, Terrell Suggs smacked Roethlisberger to the turf after a 45-yard completion to Holmes. He was briefly pulled from the game with an injured hip but returned early in the fourth quarter. Roethlisberger's five touchdown throws also gave him a career-record, single-season high of 20—in only half a season—already two more than in all of 2006. Also, by throwing a touchdown pass for his thirteenth consecutive game, he broke Bradshaw's previous team record of twelve.

Week 10 brought another victory against the Cleveland Browns, courtesy of a second-half comeback to rally from a 15-point deficit. In the 31-28 win, Roethlisberger contributed a 30-yard scramble for his own key touchdown early in the fourth quarter. Later, he made another run on an important third down, setting up a go-ahead two-yard touchdown pass to Miller. Boasting an impressive 7–2 record, Pittsburgh seemed almost certain to make the playoffs. But the following week, the

Ben Roethlisberger and Heath Miller congratulated each other after connecting for a touchdown pass in the first quarter of a game on November 5, 2007, against the Baltimore Ravens. In that contest, Roethlisberger tied a single-game Steelers' record with five touchdown passes—and all were thrown in the first half.

Steelers took a brutal pounding from the lowly New York Jets, who had a 1–8 record going into the game. The offensive line did a poor job of protecting Roethlisberger, who was sacked seven times. The game was tied at 16 at the end of regulation, but a field goal in overtime gave the Jets the 19-16 victory.

The following week, in a Monday night game, new sod plus daylong rains created the worst playing conditions ever encountered at Heinz Field or anywhere else for that matter. The Steelers broke their previous record of the lowest-scoring game in *Monday Night Football* history with a 3-0 victory over Miami. It was the first time in 64 years that an NFL game went until the final minute without any points. The last time the league witnessed a three-point game was on December 11,

1993, when the New York Jets beat Washington 3-0. Both teams had trouble running the ball—and just running. With each step, players sunk into the soggy ground. It was like running on a sandy beach. With 17 seconds left in the fourth quarter, though, Pittsburgh got close enough for Jeff Reed to kick a game-winning, 24-yard field goal. The following Sunday pumped out more rain, but this time, the sod held up. Pittsburgh canned another win, 24-10, against Cincinnati, in which Roethlisberger ran in a touchdown from six yards out and threw two touchdown passes.

The next two weeks brought the Steelers back down to Earth. A 9–3 record is pretty impressive to most teams, but perhaps not to New England. The Patriots arrived at Gillette Stadium with a flawless 12–0 record, and their play certainly matched their record. Quarterback Tom Brady's 399 passing yards dwarfed Roethlisberger's 187. A Steeler win would have clinched a playoff berth, but instead, they took a humbling 34-13 loss.

December 16 brought perfect Steelers weather—swirling snow and chilly temperatures for their warm-blooded opponents, the Jacksonville Jaguars. Still, Pittsburgh was unable to shovel out a victory, taking a 29-22 loss. Some fourth-quarter heroics, though, tempted Steeler fans into thinking a win might be possible. Down 22-7, Pittsburgh scored twice in seven-and-a-half minutes. Roethlisberger shook off a sore shoulder and five sacks to fire off three touchdown passes. Showcasing his creativity, he repeatedly improvised broken plays to make first downs. The comeback began when Anthony Smith intercepted the Jaguars' David Garrard and returned the ball 50 yards. The interception led to an 11-yard touchdown pass to Hines Ward. On the Steelers' next possession, Roethlisberger threw a 30-yard touchdown pass to Nate Washington, setting a team record with his twenty-ninth touchdown pass of the season. On a trick play, wide receiver Cedrick Wilson tossed a two-point conversion pass to Holmes to tie the game at 22 with less than six minutes remaining. Jacksonville pulled off some of their own heroics, though. Garrard directed an eight-play, 73-yard drive that ended with a 12-yard touchdown run by Fred Taylor. With just 1:57 on the clock, the Steelers could not find enough time answer it.

At 9–5, the Steelers fell into a tie with Cleveland for the AFC North lead. They needed a win on December 20 against the St. Louis Rams. They got one—a super-sized 41-24 win. The victory came with some strings attached, however. In his first carry of the game, star running back Willie Parker went down with a broken bone in his lower right leg. He would be out for the rest of the season. His replacement—Najeh Davenport—made sure his spot was well covered. He rushed for 123 yards and two touchdowns. Roethlisberger was 16 of 20 for 261 yards, with three touchdowns and no interceptions. The win was important, but the Steelers still needed a little help in order to clinch a playoff berth. Either Cleveland would have to lose at Cincinnati or the Jets would have to beat the Tennessee Titans. As it turned out, Cleveland's loss saved the day. Win or lose in Game 16, the Steelers were headed to the playoffs.

Coach Tomlin decided to enter the final game of the season with an ounce-of-prevention philosophy—stay healthy. Throughout the season, the starters had gotten pretty banged up. Tomlin wanted to use the final week before the playoffs to let his players heal, including Big Ben, who suffered a sprained ankle in St. Louis. Backup quarterback Charlie Batch put up a pretty good fight, but the Steelers lost to Baltimore 27-21 and finished the regular season with a 10–6 record. Next stop: the AFC wild-card game. "Ready or not, here we come," Tomlin said.

The Steelers' dream of making it to the Super Bowl for the second time in three years shattered just as quickly as it took shape. By the end of the first half against Jacksonville, Roethlisberger had dug the team into a deep hole with three interceptions, as the Steelers trailed 21-7. As in the earlier, regular-season game against the Jaguars, Roethlisberger led a thundering fourth-quarter rally, after switching to a shotgun formation. With vir-

After an AFC Pro Bowl practice in February 2008 in Hawaii, Ben Roethlisberger signed autographs for a group of U.S. Army soldiers. Heading into his fifth season in the NFL, Roethlisberger has had many outstanding accomplishments, and is certain to have many more.

tually no running game, Roethlisberger shouldered the offense himself. He threw touchdown passes to Santonio Holmes and Heath Miller in the first four-and-a-half minutes of the fourth quarter to bring Pittsburgh within five points, 28-23. Instead of going for the extra point, Tomlin called a two-point conversion. But Roethlisberger's pass to Ward was incomplete.

Next possession, Big Ben led another short-and-sweet touchdown drive, putting Pittsburgh ahead by one point. Once again, Tomlin opted for the two-point conversion. Again, it failed. With 37 seconds left in the game, Jaguars kicker Josh Scobee cleared a 25-yard field goal to win the game 31-29. The Steelers came up short by gambling for two-point conversions after their final two touchdowns—getting neither. In hindsight, Tomlin questioned his decisions. Perhaps it would have been better to settle for the extra point. But a team doesn't get a nickname like the "Steel Curtain" by tip-toeing its way through a football game. Even though it marked the end of the road for Pittsburgh, Roethlisberger finished off the season in good standing with a 104.1 passer rating, second only to the Patriots' Tom Brady. For Roethlisberger and the rest of the Steelers, though, there was only one thing left to do: Win it next year.

GREATEST SUPER BOWL EVER?

The 2008 season found the Steelers with the most difficult schedule in the league. Yet, early on, the team was called a Super Bowl contender by ESPN. The Steelers opened up their regular season on September 7, with a victory over the Houston Texans. They never looked back. Although he suffered several injuries during the 2008 season, Roethlisberger became the second most prolific quarterback in franchise history and his seventh playoff win moved him past Troy Aikman for second most all-time (number one is Tom Brady with nine).

With their win over the Baltimore Ravens for the AFC Championship, next came Super Bowl XLIII on February 1, 2009. The game played against the Arizona Cardinals at Raymond James Stadium in Tampa, Florida, became a contest between one of the most successful teams in the NFL against a team that had not won a championship since 1947. A lot was on the line for both teams. While this would be the Cardinals first win in 60 years, a victory for the Steelers would give them the record for most Super Bowl wins, at six. Roethlisberger was determined to atone for his performance during Super Bowl XL, where he had one of the worst passing games of his career.

On the first two offensive drives, Roethlisberger passed for 122 yards on seven of eight passing attempts, which is one yard shy of his first Super Bowl start. Going into halftime, the Steelers led 17-7 until the Cardinals mounted a comeback. The Cardinals scored 16 points in the fourth quarter to make the score 23-20. Just when it looked like the Cardinals had achieved the greatest comeback in Super Bowl history, the

Steelers rallied and made a historic play when it mattered most. With just 35 seconds left in the game, Roethlisberger threw a 6-yard touchdown pass to win it all for the Steelers, 27-23.

Not only did this game have the longest play in Super Bowl history—a 100-yard interception return for a touchdown by the Steelers linebacker James Harrison—but it has been called the most exciting Super Bowl ever. "This will go down as one of the greatest games ever played," said Steelers receiver Santonio Holmes, who caught the game-winning touchdown and finished with nine catches for 131 yards and a score. "The greatest Super Bowl ever."

In just five seasons with the Steelers, Roethlisberger has become the second most productive quarterback in franchise history (behind Terry Bradshaw). Sports broadcasters have hailed him as "the second coming of John Elway" due to this late clutch game-winning drives and the repeated sacks he has endured throughout his career. He finished the season with 3,301 passing yards and 17 touchdowns, with 15 interceptions, and currently ranks seventh with a passer rating of 93.2. A big-time talent, Roethlisberger has shown he comes through when it matters most. Two Super Bowl wins in five seasons is sure proof of this fact.

STATISTICS

BEN ROETHLISBERGER
Position: Quarterback

FULL NAME:
Benjamin Roethlisberger
BORN: March 2, 1982,
Findlay, Ohio
HEIGHT: 6'5"
HEIGHT: 240 lbs.

COLLEGE: Miami
(Ohio)
TEAMS:
Pittsburgh Steelers
(2004–present)

YEAR	TEAM	G	COMP	ATT	PCT	YD	Y/A	TD	INT
2004	PIT	14	196	295	66.4	2,621	8.9	17	11
2005	PIT	12	168	268	62.7	2,385	8.9	17	9
2006	PIT	15	280	469	59.7	3,513	7.5	18	23
2007	PIT	15	264	404	65.3	3,154	7.8	32	11
2008	PIT	16	281	469	59.9	3,301	7.0	17	15
TOTALS		72	1,189	1,905	62.4	14,974	7.9	101	69

CHRONOLOGY

1982 Is born on March 2 in Findlay, Ohio.

1999 Becomes the starting quarterback at Findlay High; sets state records for touchdowns and passing yards.

2000 Redshirts his first year at Miami University.

2001 Becomes the starting quarterback for the Miami University RedHawks; passes for 25 touchdowns and 3,105 yards for the season.

2002 Passes for 3,238 yards and 22 touchdowns for the season.

2003 Passes for 4,486 yards and 37 touchdowns for the season.

TIMELINE

1982
Is born on March 2 in Findlay, Ohio

2001
Becomes the starting quarterback for the Miami University RedHawks

2003
Leads Miami to the Mid-American Conference title

1982

2004

1999
Sets Ohio high school records for touchdowns and passing yards

2004
Drafted by the Pittsburgh Steelers in the first round

December 4 Leads Miami to its first Mid-American Conference title since 1986, defeating Bowling Green, 49-27.

December 18 Guides Miami to a 49-28 win over Louisville in the GMAC Bowl; declares he will enter the NFL Draft.

2004   April 24 Drafted by the Pittsburgh Steelers with the eleventh pick in the first round.

September 19 Makes his NFL debut when starting quarterback Tommy Maddox goes out with an injury.

September 26 Makes first NFL start; Pittsburgh beats Miami, 13-3.

2005
Wins first NFL playoff game, 20-17, over the Jets

2006
Quarterbacks the Steelers to victory in Super Bowl XL

2009
Leads the Steelers to a record six Super Bowl wins

2004

2007

2009

2004
Becomes the first NFL quarterback to compile a 13–0 record during the regular season

2006
Suffers head and facial injuries in a motorcycle accident on June 12

2007
Ties the Steelers' single-game record with five touch-down passes

BEN ROETHLISBERGER

Becomes the first NFL quarterback to compile a 13–0 record during the regular season; is named the Associated Press NFL Offensive Rookie of the Year.

2005   **January 15** Wins first NFL playoff game, 20-17, over the Jets.
January 23 Steelers lose to New England, 41-27, in the AFC Championship Game.
For the 2005 season, leads Pittsburgh to an 11–5 record.

2006   **January 22** Pittsburgh beats Denver, 34-17, to win the AFC Championship Game; Roethlisberger is the first quarterback to reach a conference championship game in each of his first two seasons in the NFL.

February 5 Pittsburgh wins Super Bowl XL, beating the Seattle Seahawks 21-10.
June 12 Fractures his jaw and suffers other head and facial injuries in a motorcycle accident.
September 3 Undergoes an emergency appendectomy; forced to miss the Steelers' season opener. The Steelers finish 8–8 for the season and miss the playoffs.

2007   Bill Cowher steps down after 15 season as the coach of the Steelers; Pittsburgh names Mike Tomlin as his replacement.
November 5 Ties the Steelers' single-game record with five touchdown passes, in a game against the Ravens. Pittsburgh finishes the season with a 10–6 record but loses to Jacksonville in the first round of the playoffs.

2008   **March** Signs eight-year contract extension worth $102 million, making him one of the NFL's highest paid players.

2009   **February 1** With just 35 seconds to go in the game, Roethlisberger throws a 6-yard touchdown pass to win Super Bowl XLIII, beating the Cardinals 27–23. The Steelers hold the record for most Super Bowl titles, with six.

GLOSSARY

American Football Conference (AFC)   One of the two conferences in the National Football League (NFL). The AFC was established after the NFL merged with the American Football League (AFL) in 1970.

blind side   The side opposite the direction a player is looking. For example, when a right-handed quarterback sets up to pass, his left side is considered his blind side.

blitz   A defensive tactic in which the linebacker or defensive back abandons his normal duties on the field and goes after the quarterback; his objective is either to tackle the quarterback behind the line of scrimmage or rush the quarterback's pass.

bootleg   An offensive play in which a quarterback fakes a handoff to a running back who is going in one direction while he moves in the opposite direction to run or pass.

bye week   A week in which one team does not play.

coach's challenge   When a coach disagrees with a ruling on the field, he can challenge it by tossing a red flag before the next play starts; the play is reviewed by the referee, who decides if the call stands; if the challenge fails, the challenging team is charged with a timeout.

cornerback   A defensive back who lines up near the line of scrimmage across from a wide receiver. The cornerback's primary job is to disrupt passing routes, to defend against short and medium passes, and to contain the rusher on rushing plays.

depth chart   A list of all players on a team's roster, with rankings from starter to second- and third-string players.

draft   The selection of collegiate players for entrance into the National Football League. Typically, the team with the worst record over the previous season picks first in the draft.

draw play   A disguised run that at first looks like a pass play; the offensive linemen fake as if they are going to pass-block, and the quarterback drops back as if he is going to throw a pass, but instead he turns and hands off to a running back or runs himself.

end zone   The area between the end line and the goal line, bounded by the sidelines.

extra point   After a touchdown, the scoring team is allowed to add another point by kicking the football through the uprights of the goalpost.

field goal   A scoring play worth three points if the placekicker can boot the ball between the uprights of the goalpost.

first down   The first of a set of four downs. Usually, a team that has a first down needs to advance the ball 10 yards to receive another first down, but penalties or field position (i.e. less than 10 yards from the opposing end zone) can affect this.

flat   The area of the field between the hash marks and the sideline near the line of scrimmage.

fourth down   The final of a set of four downs. Unless a first down is achieved or a penalty forces a replay of the down, the team will lose control of the ball after this play. If a team does not think it can get a first down, it will often punt on fourth down or kick a field goal if close enough to do so.

fumble   When any offensive player loses possession of the ball before the play is blown dead.

Hail Mary   An offensive play in which the quarterback throws the ball without really targeting a specific receiver, hoping someone on his team will catch the ball. Typically, a Hail Mary pass is used on the last play of the half or the game, when a team is out of field-goal range and has time left for only one play.

interception   A pass that is caught by a defensive player, giving his team the ball.

lateral   A sideways or backward pass.

ligament   A sheet or band of tough, fibrous tissue that connects bones or cartilage at a joint or that holds an organ of the body in place.

line of scrimmage   The imaginary line that stretches across the field and separates the two teams before the snap; before a play, teams line up on either side of the line of scrimmage.

move the chains   Using first downs to drive a team, play by play, toward their opponent's end zone.

National Football Conference (NFC)   One of the two conferences in the National Football League (NFL). The NFC was established after the NFL merged with the American Football League (AFL) in 1970.

offensive line   The offensive players who line up on the line of scrimmage. Their primary job is to block the defensive players.

onside kick   An attempt by the kicking team to recover the ball by kicking it a short distance down the field. An onside kick must go 10 yards before a player on the kicking team can touch the ball.

passer rating   (also **quarterback rating**) A numeric value used to measure the performance of quarterbacks. It was formulated in 1973, and it uses the player's completion percentage, passing yards, touchdowns, and interceptions.

plane   An imaginary screen that extends upward from the goal line. If the football "breaks the plane" by passing over the goal line, a touchdown is scored, even if the player carrying the football is pulled back.

pocket   The area of protection for the quarterback that is formed by the offensive line when he drops back to pass.

quarterback   The offensive player who receives the ball from the center at the start of each play. The quarterback will hand off the ball, pass the ball, or run it himself.

redshirt   A college player who skips a year of play without losing a year of eligibility. College athletes are only eligible to play for four years. A player will often redshirt because of an injury or an academic problem.

reverse   A play in which a running back takes a handoff from the quarterback and then turns and runs in a lateral motion behind the line of scrimmage before handing off to a receiver who is running in the opposite direction.

rookie   A player in his first year as a professional.

roughing the passer   Purposely hitting or running into the quarterback after the ball has been passed; this penalty can also be called if the quarterback is hit in the head.

rush   To run with the ball

sack   A tackle of the quarterback behind the line of scrimmage.

screen pass   A forward pass to a receiver at or behind the line of scrimmage who is protected by a screen of blockers.

secondary   The defensive players who line up behind the linebackers and defend the pass.

seed   A team's rank in the playoffs.

shotgun offense   A passing formation in which the quarterback stands five yards behind the center before the snap; the shotgun allows a quarterback to scan the defense from behind the line of scrimmage.

shovel pass   A short, underhanded pass.

slant pattern   A play in which the ball carrier runs at an angle across the field instead of running straight toward the end zone.

signing bonus   An amount of money a player receives just to sign with a team.

snap   The act when the center throw or hands the ball to the quarterback, or to the holder on a kick, or to the punter.

special teams   The group of players on the field during kicks, punts, and extra points.

swing pass   A route used by running backs as they "swing" out of the backfield; they break left or right of the line of scrimmage and then begin to head downfield. These passes are often caught in the flat.

tendon   A tough cord or band of dense white fibrous connective tissue that unites a muscle with some other part (like a bone) and transmits the force that the muscle exerts.

tight end   A player position on offense, who lines up on the line of scrimmage next to the offensive tackle. Tight ends are used as blockers during running plays and either run a route or stay in to block during passing plays.

touchdown   A play worth six points in which any part of the ball while legally in the possession of a player crosses the plane of the opponent's goal line. A touchdown allows the team a chance for one extra point by kicking the ball or a two-point conversion.

turnover   The loss of possession due to a fumble or an interception.

two-point conversion   A scoring play immediately after a touchdown during which a team can add two points to the score instead kicking for just one point; in a two-point conversion, the scoring team has one play to run or pass the ball into the end zone from the opponent's 2-yard line.

wideout   A player position on offense, also known as a wide receiver. He is split wide (usually about 10 yards) from the formation and plays on the line of scrimmage as a split end or one yard off as a flanker.

wild card   The two playoff spots given to the two non-division winning teams that have the best records in the conference

BIBLIOGRAPHY

Associated Press. "Drained Bills Lose First Game Since Everett's Injury." ESPN.com, September 16, 2007.

———. "Rossum's Return TD, Parker's Ground Game Lift Steelers." ESPN.com, September 23, 2007.

———. "Banged-Up Steelers Lose Parker in Win at Green Bay." ESPN.com, November 6, 2005.

———. "Batch, Maddox, Randle El Combine at QB for Steeler Win." ESPN.com, November 13, 2005.

———. "Ben Apologizes, Pledges He'll Ride Wearing a Helmet." ESPN.com, June 16, 2006.

———. "Big Ben Sacked Nine Times, Steelers Blanked by Ravens." ESPN.com, November 26, 2006.

———. "Bengals Denied Playoff Berth After OT Loss to Steelers, 0-3 Finish." ESPN.com, December 31, 2006.

———. "Bengals' Conservative Play Sets Tone for Defeat vs. Steelers." ESPN.com, October 28, 2007.

———. "Bettis Carries Load for 129 Yards." ESPN.com, November 21, 2004.

———. "Bettis's Passing TD, Rushing Score Power Pittsburgh." ESPN.com, December 12, 2004.

———. "Bettis, Steelers Snap Bears' Eight-Game Win Streak." ESPN.com, December 11, 2005.

———. "Big Ben Has Big Letdown Against Opportunistic Raiders." ESPN.com, October 29, 2006.

———. "Big Ben's Heroics Help Pittsburgh Escape Cleveland." ESPN.com, November 19, 2006.

———. "Big Ben Returns in Steelers' 10th Straight Road Win." ESPN.com, October 23, 2005.

———. "Big Ben Turns to Gentle Ben in Steelers' Loss," ESPN.com, January 23, 2005.

———. "Big Ben, Davenport Power Steelers to Victory." ESPN. com, October 7, 2007.

———."Brady Completes Last 12 Passes to Rally Patriots." ESPN.com, September 25, 2005.

———. "Broncos Prove Mistake-Prone Steelers Super No More." ESPN.com, November 5, 2006.

———. "Brownout: Steelers Defense Dominates in 41-0 Rout." ESPN.com, December 24, 2005.

———. "Cardinals Shut Down Steelers' High-Scoring Offense." ESPN.com, September 30, 2007.

———. "Davenport Replaces Injured Parker, Rushes Steelers to Victory." ESPN.com, December 20, 2007.

———. "Deion Tweaks Hammy in Win." ESPN.com, September 19, 2004.

———. "Dolphins Continue Woeful Ways, Fall to 0-11 After Sloppy Game." ESPN.com, November 26, 2007.

———. "Elam's Last-Second Field Goal Dumps Steelers." ESPN.com, October 21, 2007.

———. "Fourth-Down Stop Gives Pittsburgh Momentum." ESPN.com, September 26, 2004.

———. "Fresh Batch: QB Sparks Steelers Past Dolphins in Opener." ESPN.com, September 7, 2006.

———. "Jaguars Devour Steelers in Lowest-Scoring MNF Game Ever." ESPN.com, September 18, 2006.

———. "Jaguars Relinquish 18-Point Lead but Stun Steelers at End." ESPN.com, January 5, 2008.

———. "Manning Throws Two TDs As Colts Stay Perfect." ESPN.com, November 28, 2005.

———. "McGahee Keeps It Close, but Bills Fall Short." ESPN. com, January 2, 2005.

———. "McNair, Ravens Deal Fatal Blow to Steelers' Playoff Hopes." ESPN.com, December 24, 2006.

———. "Nugent Nails 38-Yard FG to Lift Jets Past Steelers in OT." ESPN.com, November 18, 2007.

———. "Palmer Gets Measure of Revenge Against Steelers." ESPN.com, September 24, 2006.

———. "Palmer, Bengals Hand Reeling Steelers Third Straight Loss." ESPN.com, December 4, 2005.

———. "Parker Breaks Steelers' Single-Game Record with 223 Rushing Yards." ESPN.com, December 7, 2006.

———. "Parker Fuels Steelers' Rout of Reeling Panthers." ESPN.com, December 17, 2006.

———. "Parker Runs Wild (213 Yards) As Steelers Rally to Beat Saints." ESPN.com, November 12, 2006.

———. "Parker-Roethlisberger Combo Overwhelms Titans." ESPN.com, September 11, 2005.

———. "Patriots Put Bruising on Steelers, Become 5th Team with 13-0 Mark." ESPN.com, December 9, 2007.

———. "Pittsburgh Continues Longest Winning Streak Since '76." ESPN.com, November 28, 2004.

———. "Polamalu Intercepts Ex-College Roommate to Seal Win." ESPN.com, October 3, 2004.

———. "Ravens Break Skid with Win over Indifferent Steelers." ESPN.com, December 30, 2007.

———. "Ravens Snap Four-Game Skid with OT Win vs. Steelers." ESPN.com, November 20, 2005.

———. "Reed's 19th Straight Made Field Goal Gives Pittsburgh Win." ESPN.com, January 15, 2005.

———. "Reed's 37-Yard Field Goal with 18 Ticks Left Wins It." ESPN.com, December 5, 2004.

———. "Rivers, Chargers Send Steelers to Third Straight Loss." ESPN.com, October 8, 2006.

———. "Roethlisberger First Rookie QB 4-0 Since '79." ESPN. com, October 17, 2004.

———. "Roethlisberger Passes for Career Best 316 Yards," ESPN.com, December 18, 2004.

———. "Roethlisberger Remains Unbeaten." ESPN.com, October 31, 2004.

———. "Roethlisberger Signs Long-Term Deal." SI.com, March 3, 2008.

———. "Roethlisberger Takes Third Straight Win." ESPN.com, October 10, 2004.

———."Roethlisberger Tosses Career-High Four TDs in Rout of Browns." ESPN.com, September 9, 2007.

———. "Roethlisberger Uses Legs to Lead Steelers Past Browns." ESPN.com, November 11, 2007.

———. "Rookie Miller Catches 2 TDs in Steelers' Win over Ravens." ESPN.com, October 31, 2005.

———. "Steelers Click on Both Sides of the Ball, Dominate the Ravens at Home." ESPN.com, November 5, 2007.

———. "Steelers First to Win Three on Road to Reach Super Bowl Since 1985." January 22, 2006.

———. "Steelers Get Big Defensive Effort in Road Win over Vikings." ESPN.com, December 18, 2005.

———. "Steelers Get Past Seahawks for Fifth Super Bowl Win in Club History." ESPN.com, February 5, 2006.

———. "Steelers Rally to Beat Chargers; Big Ben Hurt." ESPN. com, October 10, 2005.

———. "Steelers Ride Three Bus Touchdowns into Playoffs." ESPN.com, January 1, 2006.

———. "Steelers Survive as Colts Attempt to Tie Sails Wide." ESPN.com, January 15, 2006.

———. "Steelers Use Buccaneers' Turnovers to Their Advantage." ESPN.com, December 3, 2006.

———. "Steelers Win 7th Straight; Bettis Runs for 103." ESPN.com, November 14, 2004.

———. "Steelers Win Eighth Straight Road Game." ESPN.com, September 18, 2005.

———. "Steelers Wrap Up Home-Field Advantage Throughout Playoffs," ESPN.com, December 26, 2004.

———. "Taylor's 12-Yard TD Run in Final Two Minutes Wins It for Jags." ESPN.com, December 16, 2007.

———. "They're Back: Steel Curtain Drops on Kansas City." ESPN.com, October 15, 2006.

———. "Unbeaten? Steelers Make It Look Easy—Again." ESPN.com, November 7, 2004.

———. "Vick Fires 4 TDs as Falcons KO Steelers, Big Ben in OT." ESPN.com, October 22, 2006.

———. "Ward's Two TD Help Steelers Dump Bengals at Home." ESPN.com, December 2, 2007.

———. "Without Palmer, Bengals Struggle, Fall to Steelers." ESPN.com, January 8, 2006.

———. "Without Roethlisberger, Ward, Steelers Fall to Jags." ESPN.com, October 16, 2005.

Attner, Paul. "Above a Cut: Steelers Rookie Ben Roethlisberger Is the Gem Among a Group of Four Young Quarterbacks Who Are Providing an Influx of Refreshing New Talent at the NFL's Marquee Position." *Sporting News*, November 22, 2004.

Bouchette, Ed. "Big Ben Says First Year Under Tomlin Proof NFL Offensive Trends Aren't Passing Steelers By." *Pittsburgh Post-Gazette*. January 17, 2008.

ESPN.com. "Big Ben in Serious Condition after Motorcycle Accident." ESPN.com, June 13, 2006.

Kremer, Andrea. "Roethlisberger in 2005—'The Safest Rider I Can Be'," July 2005, updated on ESPN.com June 12, 2006.

Maske, Mark. "Roethlisberger Hurt in Crash." *The Washington Post*, June 13, 2006.

McNellie, Tim. "Big Ben's Beguiling Boldness." *Washington Crossroad*, December 2006.

Merron, Jeff. "Taking Your Wonderlics." ESPN.com.

Passquarelli, Len. "Cowher Set to Quit As Steelers' Coach After 15 Seasons." ESPN.com, January 5, 2007.

Pittsburgh Tribune-Review. *Tough as Steel: Pittsburgh Steelers, 2006 Super Bowl Champions*. Champaign, Ill.: Tribune-Review Publishing Company/Sports Publishing L.L.C., 2006.

Silver, Michael. "Ben There, Done That." *Sports Illustrated*. November 8, 2004.

Sports Publishing L.L.C. *Roethlisberger: Pittsburgh's Own Big Ben*. Champaign, Ill.: Sports Publishing L.L.C., 2004.

Starkey, Joe. "Tomlin Deflects Controversy with Easy Manner." ESPN.com. May 15, 2007.

Wilbon, Michael. "On the Big Stage, This One Is Nothing to Sing About." *The Washington Post*, February 5, 2005.

Zenor, John. "Louisville Stopped by RedHawks in GMAC Bowl." UofLsports.com.

FURTHER READING

BOOKS

Bettis, Jerome. *The Bus: My Life In and Out of a Helmet*. New York: Doubleday, 2007.

Grdnic, Dale. *Pittsburgh Steelers: Glory Days*. Champaign, IL: Sports Publishing L.L.C., 2007.

Mendelson, Abby. *Pittsburgh Steelers 3rd Edition: The Official Team History*. Lanham, Md.: Taylor Trade Publishing, Distributed by National Book Network, 2006.

Rooney, Dan. *Dan Rooney: My 75 Years with the Pittsburgh Steelers and the NFL*. New York: Da Capo Press, 2007.

Wexall, Jim. *Pittsburgh Steelers: Men of Steel*. Champaign, Ill.: Sports Publishing L.L.C., 2006.

Pittsburgh Tribune-Review. *Tough as Steel: Pittsburgh Steelers 2006 Super Bowl Champions*. Champaign, Ill.: Tribune-Review Publishing Company/Sports Publishing L.L.C., 2006.

Sports Publishing L.L.C. *Roethlisberger: Pittsburgh's Own Big Ben*. Champaign, Ill.: Sports Publishing L.L.C., 2004.

WEB SITES

Big Ben 7: The Official Site of Ben Roethlisberger
www.bigben7.com

The NFL on ESPN.com
http://sports-ak.espn.go.com/nfl/index

The Official Site of the National Football League
www.nfl.com

The Official Site of the Pittsburgh Steelers
www.steelers.com

The Official Web Site of Jerome "The Bus" Bettis
www.thebus36.com

PICTURE CREDITS

INDEX

130

ABOUT THE AUTHOR

RACHEL A. KOESTLER-GRACK has worked with nonfiction books as an editor and writer since 1999. During her career, she has worked extensively with historical topics, ranging from the Middle Ages to the Colonial era to the civil rights movement. In addition, she has written numerous biographies on a variety of historical and contemporary figures. Rachel lives with her husband and daughter in the German community of New Ulm, Minnesota.